FRONT OF THE LIN

Adventures with the Irish Brigade

To the Infantry

who, as they grovelled and prayed in the ditch, touched the hand of God

The Irish Brigade

6th (later 2nd) Royal Inniskilling Fusiliers (The Skins)
2nd London Irish Rifles (The Rifles)
1st Royal Irish Fusiliers (The Faughs)

Of whom some 1,000 lie somewhere between Dunkirk and Belgrade

For it's always to be seen,
The shamrock and the green,
In front of the thin, red line.

FRONT OF THE LINE

Adventures with the Irish Brigade

Colin J. Gunner

with a foreword by Philip Larkin

Editor:
Richard Doherty

GREYSTONE BOOKS

1991

First published 1991
Greystone Books Ltd., Antrim, Northern Ireland

ISBN 1 870157 14 1

Cover: Rodney Miller Associates, Belfast

Typeset by Textflow Services Ltd., Belfast
Printed in Northern Ireland by W. & G. Baird Ltd.

List of Contents

Preface

A BOOK already provided with a foreword by Philip Larkin should require no introduction. The poet, however, did not soldier with the author. So I have accepted the privilege of writing these lines about a courageous and resilient young Englishman of distinct character who has to this day never forgotten his allegiance to a formidable Irish regiment.

I hold that same allegiance and, as current chairman of the Regimental Trustees of The Royal Irish Fusiliers, I thank Colin for his notable services to the Regiment, in war and peace. There are not many officers who, after a detachment from their Battalion, have been greeted on the battlefield with a cheer from their old platoon; Colin is one.

Finally, were he still alive, Sir Arthur Bryant would be very pleased to learn of the publication of this book for, back in the '70s, he wrote to the author '. . . I like that book of yours . . . very much . . . I should like to see your testimony published, for it deserves to be'.

Brian Clark*

---

* Lieutenant Colonel Brian Clark is a holder of the Military Cross and the George Medal. [Editor]

Foreword

THE KEY to this book appears on an early page. Colin Gunner, having decided to anticipate his call-up by volunteering, is duly sworn-in at the Recruiting Office and given a day's pay of five shillings. He stares at the two half-crowns with dissatisfaction. Where was the King's shilling? he protests, at first in vain, at length ('Quite right – the lad's entitled to one – get one at once, sergeant') with success: he leaves the room with two florins and the precious shilling. 'It hangs in my room still, unspent'.

This account of where that shilling led him contrasts vividly with other, more disillusioned narratives, for Colin Gunner's love affair with the Army never came to an end. Not that he had an easy war. In consequence of another gesture in the face of authority ('any infantry regiment of the line'), he, a Coventry boy of middle-class background, became attached to the kind of Irish regiment that, along with the Scottish and Commonwealth troops, gets thrown into action whenever the going is tough. He seems (I cannot claim to have mastered completely the almost illegible typescript he sent me) to have been posted from Catterick to North Africa and then to Italy, where he was to fight his way up to Monte Cassino and see the end of the war. Ice, mud, danger, dysentery, all came his way. Yet his enthusiasm did not dwindle. It is hard to analyse its source. Much is owed to the fellowship of comrades-in-arms, especially the Irish, who were new to him. Much arises from day-to-day humour of an elementary kind; the officer begging assistance to be catapulted into a cesspit, the commandeered motorcycle, the sad tale of the man who rented an apartment in Cairo.

The fact that it was his war service that first awoke his interest in the Roman Catholic Church, ('a twenty-one year old, non-church-going, nominal Protestant') no doubt counts for much. At bottom, however, it is the glamour of that shilling that keeps him going; it is the historical tradition of the British Army, the drinking, the scrounging, the deserting, the endurance, the courage, all going back to the First World War, the campaigns of Edward and Victoria, to Waterloo and the Peninsular, all these seem to support him at the darkest moments. In the Second World War such sentiments were rare.

One might conclude from this that Gunner is a romantic, but this is not my recollection of him – for I must admit, and should perhaps have done so earlier, that we were schoolfellows. In fact he stays in my memory as quite the reverse: I remember him, on the day when, in common with all school-children, we had been presented with a George VI coronation mug, shying his into that squalid sewer, the River Sowe (I have mine still). Perhaps he was a King's man, a supporter of Edward VIII; for me the action proclaimed him iconoclast and sceptic. We first met in the Junior School of King Henry VIII School, Coventry, in the early 1930s – or was it the first form of the school itself? It was certainly before the traumatic influx of scholarship boys in the second form, and the start of Latin and French; he was sitting next to me when Jimmy Mattocks took us through *The Wind in the Willows* (missing out the chapters about Mole's old home, and Pan, and Rat's wish to emigrate), and he was there when we played cricket in white shorts (as opposed to white longs), and bowled fast. I remember him, and indeed school photographs bear this out, as a small, agile, tough boy, with a face like a nut, very much at home in the world of Bassett-Lowke, Warnford, and Rudge-Whitworth, and whose home background seemed, if not richer than mine, at least more sophisti-cated; his parents had a car.

At that time I was not happy at school. Admittedly it was an affair of being more frightened than hurt, but it was being hurt sometimes, and being frightened was not very pleasant. And in any case it was an affair of being more bored than either. The very words physics, geography, algebra, chemis-try still conjure up in my mind a pantheon of tedium, and handicapped by not being able to see the blackboard (I never said anything about this, and nobody ever noticed it). The one compensation was the discovery that Colin and I could make each other almost hysterical with laughter by weaving fantasies about the extraordinary characters that daily stood before us, roaring, scratch-ing, gesturing, glowering – Knobby, Beaky, Squiffy, Pansy, Majack, Wooly Willy and the rest. The grotesque and memorable tapestry to which we added daily at break, or walking down Warwick Road after school, derived from a variety of sources: *The Magnet*, certainly, and *Tom Brown's Schooldays*, but also films such as *Dracula* and the more colourful aspects of the Hitler regime. I don't pretend that such inventions are uncommon, and I certainly have no intention of detailing ours in particular; all I say is that they made school bearable for me. Ironically, Colin was supposed to be a 'bad influence' in my school life; presumably my teachers thought that without him at my elbow I should have done better in class (my form position was always well down in the twenties). But in fact we were developing our imaginations independently of the School Certificate syllabus, and if anything were to be envied rather than reprimanded. Later on, we used to meet at the Central Library in the evenings, at the foot of the as-yet-unbombed cathedral, emerging (in my case) with literary biographies and argumentative books about religion, and (in Colin's) military and regimental history.

Colin had, as far as I know, no literary ambitions, but he was a natural writer, and I think this book shows as much. His English essays came back with 'Vigorous' written at the bottom, though an attempt to apply the same technique to physics questions ('Bzzzz! When we hear the familiar summons of the electric bell, do we ever pause to reflect on the intricacies of the mechanism that, etc') evoked caustic comment from the Mad Undergrad, as we called the physics master. On the basis of this talent, he planned to join the *Midland Daily Telegraph*, as it was then, but this intention was thwarted when he failed his School Certificate. This seems to me now, as it did then, a great injustice.

Such recollections make it difficult for me to introduce this book dispassionately, for so much of it is Colin in his habit as he lived, gay, rhetorical, courageous, sentimental, always ready with a quotation, never too subservient to the rules of punctuation or orthography. It reminds me of the creeping tedium of morning and afternoon school, the consultation of one's (usually new) watch, the grins exchanged across the classroom when the master in charge innocently made some remark that chimed with his Dickensian, or Rowlandsonian, life-style that we had devised for him. But if I look at these pages with the eye of a stranger, I am still bound to acknowledge the helter-skelter of incident, the vivacity of detail, the always-present but never-laboured humour, and the equanimity with which their author encounters and relates a set of experiences which, even if, like the Clerk of the Court in *The Wind in the Willows*, one believes only one-tenth of them, must have been more than usually shattering. The claims I would make for Colin's narrative refer more to temperament than to texture; here is someone meeting unpleasant events with insouciance and endurance, and above all a tactful modesty; and yet if the writing were not an extraordinary blend of unpretentiousness with complete confidence it would not be – as, in my view, it is – immensely readable.

Philip Larkin
1973

Chapter 1

The King's Shilling

In 1941 the British Army was engaged in North Africa while Germany had just attacked Russia. The evacuation from Dunkirk was in the past and there was a greater feeling of optimism in the air. It was against this background that the young Colin Gunner volunteered to join the Army.

So CATTERICK it was to be. After some weeks of waiting and guessing, I held the slip of paper ordering me to report to 'Officer Commanding 56th Training Regiment, Royal Armoured Corps' at Catterick Camp. It had seemed a difficult goal to achieve at times. Together with Dennis Newman, my travelling companion to the Aldershot of the North, I had helped to mismanage small affairs in a local motor car company in the months between the clang of the school leaving gate and the clack of the Birmingham train. My parents had come to realise that I would go eventually, but with memories of the Somme and the Ypres Salient never far away, merely stressed again and again 'Just so long as it's not the infantry'. Perhaps it was then, during those admonitions, that I knew that it had to be the infantry one day, despite watching many of my older school fellows swagger away in the glories of bandolier, breeches and spurs of the Warwickshire Yeomanry.

The infantry lurked down in the pit of the thoughts – what had Sassoon, read at the age of 15, said? – something about 'going out gardening with a tiger loose in the shrubbery'. Newman and I had solved our mutual problems by going together to the local recruiting office and simply asking them to have us in the army. They seemed a bit taken aback, and having looked at our respective heights and ruled out the Guards, suggested the Armoured Corps. We both digested the idea and eventually found ourselves holding a Bible and swearing away for the duration. We were then passed to an aged sergeant, who gave us the five shillings allowed for our day's 'maintenance'.

Here and then I jibbed for the first time in my military career. I had received two half-crowns. I demanded the King's Shilling. None was to be had, money was money, anyway 'This wasn't Kipling's army, son'. I stuck to my guns and my visions of Lord Roberts. The recruiting officer, Major Vickers-Jones, a neighbour of ours, heard the discussion and came down heavily in my favour. 'Quite right – the lad's entitled to one. Get one at once,

1

Author with Sergeant Johnny Bowley of the Kensingtons (Author's Photo)

Sergeant'. I emerged, as did Newman, with two florins and my shilling. It hangs in my room still, unspent.

The Catterick-bound huddled together on Richmond Station, being sorted out by NCOs of the various arms. 'Royal Signals this way – Royal Artillery over here – anyone for the Sappers in your lot? – this way, lad'. We of the 56th Royal Armoured were about thirty in number, mostly from the Midlands, all clutching a small suitcase (shaving kit, hankies, and for the optimists, pyjamas), and all filled with trepidation. We climbed the tailboard of the first of thousands of lorries, and in the driving snow entered the Menin Lines. It was the winter of 1941, and I was aged nineteen.

As with all recruits since Alexander found his hoplites a bit under strength, the first two days were a blur. A blur of evil-smelling battle dress, boots made from mahogany, latrines, the route to the dining-hall, and the Army's great receptionist – the doctor's needle. No splendid figure in beret and binoculars leaned from the turret of his metallic chariot and bade us welcome, only 'Get fell in and hold up your arm for the officer', while Corporal Christie accepted cigarettes and showed us how to fold our blankets. Still, there was a bugle in the Guardroom and it blew the cavalry Reveille. That made up for something.

We realised that the blur was clearing when, with throbbing, microbe-laden arms, we moved all our kit to a new and bedless hut, and drew biscuits to take our rest upon the floor. Old huts of the·H pattern, the connecting bar being composed of six latrines and ten wash-basins. Huts with the cynical inscription over the door, '18 Other Ranks, 1 NCO.' We certainly had one NCO but forty of us lived in that hut. No beds or hot water came our way from that moment until we left the Menin Lines. Into the hut came a major figure in our lives – Drill Corporal Griffiths. He soon got to know us, and it took us no time at all to fear him. Stories of him abounded, and we found that we were objects of sympathy to squads under the tutelage of more amiable corporals. He was a cavalry regular of the old sabre squadron breed, aged about thirty, and had learned his discipline behind the stables from rough-riding sergeants. A squad of teenaged, civilian volunteers was a squalid insult to his code.

Hanging from the iron girders of the barrack room until ordered down, or running round the square at the *present*, soon became familiar. He had no favourites – all were equally contemptible in his eyes, but as a drill corporal he was superb. We learnt to drill, and we learnt to obey and obey damn quickly. Those girders were very hard on the palms of the hands after three minutes.

His language was unequalled by any NCO I met then, or ever. He could, at a range of two inches, deliver into one's face, a stream of undiluted, blasphemous abuse which terrified me and my fellows. Hodson, a clergyman's son in the troop, was reduced to tears on several occasions. He even confided to me in the Church Army Canteen one night that he was considering reporting Griffiths for his language. I shunned Hodson for days to avoid implication, should this event ever transpire. He did not report anything.

When the snow stopped drill, we formed the chain gang and shovelled it off the square, off the roads and the Tank Park, and on one glorious day of liberty we were taken in lorries to move it off the runways at Scorton airfield. But mainly we drilled, and drilled again. Some of us were due for our first guard soon and now had an eye cocked anxiously on the Guardroom, where dwelt an even bigger menace than Griffiths. He was a leviathan of ingenious torments – Provost Sergeant Casey.

When scurrying from the hut to the Church Army, opposite the gates, we added ten minutes to our journey to avoid passing Satan's lair. Once, when snow-bashing, I had leant on my shovel and tried to get a sodden Woodbine to draw. A scream like a leopard in a gin-trap brought me panting to the Guardroom steps, where the Prince of Darkness in person informed me that any more idling of that sort would earn me a broader picture of the cells. I shovelled no more snow that afternoon since it will not stop on a red-hot shovel, but disappears in a cloud of steam.

The guard roster went up, and I drew Guard Orderly and was congratulated all round on my fortune. No parading for inspection, no standing freezing on the gate at 2 am, no turning out for the Orderly Officer. Just roll up in fatigue dress, sweep the Guardroom, run the errands, fetch the food, and given a cushy Guard commander, get a good night's rest. So it all fell out until the door flew open at Reveille, and Casey flung a pile of equipment on the floor with a curt 'Clean it'. Whilst I performed this task, he looked up from his table and said 'Get the breakfast.'

Breakfast was duly fetched and served to the Guard. He then added 'Get the prisoners' food', and, armed with his chit, I drew breakfast for fourteen prisoners. Back across the square I trotted. One pail of tea, one tin of soya links and dried egg, one of bread and one of porridge. Without comment, Casey heaved the whole lot into the tea pail and ordered 'Serve it out'. Now I was really scared. Prisoners in the cells were reputed to be toughies and the thought of some big scouse's fist in my teeth caused some cold shivers. Thankfully, I saw that Casey was coming with me to open the cells one at a time. As I doled out a mess tin full of the swill to each, I tried to mutter an apology to excuse myself from future vengeance. No one seemed to blame me, and one grunted 'That's okay mate, I know who does it'.

The Guard was dismounted and I went back to Hut 11, and Griffiths, with a light heart, and an abiding fear of cells. Later, a rumour ran through the barracks that Casey had fallen foul of a Canadian sergeant in the Mess and that the Canadian had floored him. Never can that great Dominion have stood higher in the hearts of any regiment of the Crown than then.

*The Colonel: Lt Col John Horsfall, DSO, MC and Bar who commanded both 1st
Royal Irish Fusiliers and 2nd London Irish Rifles in the Irish Brigade (Author)*

Chapter 2

Volunteers and Conscripts

Conditions were harsh in an Army that had expanded greatly in the midst of war and many areas of Britain were taken over as training grounds. Most of them seemed to be out of the way and desolate!

THE TROOP was mainly Brummie in origin and all volunteers. Later, we were lumped in with a troop of conscripts from Bristol, but all got on well together in the end. Several were commissioned, about a third fell in action, or were wounded between the Desert and Berlin, mainly in armoured regiments. Some were decorated, a few ran away. McComish, from the Islands, was posted to The Black Watch, where his Gaelic would stand him in good stead. Going to the infantry as I did, I lost touch with all, except when as happened, I heard of a name that seemed familiar, and made enquiries. Certainly, we all grumbled at times, but never did bad blood show. All background soon ironed out under the system and if I ever paused to think that I slept between a son of one of Dunlop's directors and a slaughterer's apprentice, it never mattered, except that the apprentice had more cigarettes from home.

A son of one of the great cigarette families lived in a nearby hut, and was reputed to return from leave in a chauffeur-driven Rolls, armed with 5,000 of the family product. Somewhere up in D Squadron was Bill Conners (Cassandra of the *Mirror*). One saw very little home-sickness or crying to sleep, one saw a lot of high spirits and schoolboy wrestling on the barrack room floor. There was little selfishness and much sharing of cakes from home.

Few, if any, drank and few could afford it anyway. The red letter night in the Salvation or Church Army was treacle tart and tea. The day off was Sandes' Soldiers' Home and the cinema in camp centre. I felt sorry for an officer leaving the Club who met the cinema crowd. His right arm needed attention before he reached his Mess. We all passed off the square together, all did our specialist training in driving, gunnery and wireless. All shivered on the moors, digging out bogged Valentine tanks at 2 am, all saluted the Bandmaster and were rebuked for doing so. All treasured the moment when the RSM, on Adjutant's Parade, slipped on a patch of ice in front of the band. All learned humility, that quality which an army must drive into its recruits, and to recognise that some are set above us, some are bigger, better looking, or have three stripes. Some can say 'Come,' – and he cometh. The public schoolboys learnt it quickest, but their backsides had been kicked early in life. Remarque called it the solidarity of convicts. Major Lowsley Williams (Lousy Bill) called it 'esprit de corps' to a puzzled squadron. All were somehow crystallised at Sunday supper. Sunday was Church Parade (compulsory), then a dinner which was not bolted down to get a fag in before next parade.

The afternoon was, for the stony-broke majority, peace and fug in the barrack room under the blankets, then the stroll to the Mess Hall where the cooks had left out buns, bread, pickles and spam. We could help ourselves and cocoa supplies were generous. No orderly sergeant crashed his cane on the table demanding 'Any complaints?', no cook corporal glared at dirty hands. With knives stuck upright in the table to signify repletion, we could 'talk about our rations and a lot of other things'. It was, above all, warm and familiar.

After the sprint through the cold, the lights of Hut 11 seemed like the lights of home, but by then it had *become* home. The past was getting blurred now. The same old crack 'Going dahn now, Sir', the same scrape of a matchbox, the glow of fag ends. The same notes across the starlit square of the loveliest call of them all, notes that touched the toughest heart. The same Lights Out.

Chapter 3

The Officer Cadet

Colin Gunner is identified as 'officer material' and sent to a Selection Board; he decides that he wants to be an infantry officer.

FROM CATTERICK I went to Blackdown OCTU to face the three-day trial by Selection Board. While at Blackdown I realised, as did my Troop Officer, that tanks and I were not compatible. Too much technical stuff I thought. Would Patton or Allenby have been so upset if I did not know the name of the cog wheel which made the track go round? Blackdown was upset, so at the final interview at the Selection Board, I jibbed again. This last interview was with the hitherto unseen presence, the Commandant. I firmly wrote on the questionnaire which asked, that if considered, to which regiment we would ask to be commissioned, the words 'Any infantry Regiment of the Line'.

We were then marched one at a time into Jehovah's office. After causing the inkwell to jump on his desk with my salute, I gazed fixedly over his head and heard a voice ask why, since I was in the Tanks, I had asked for the infantry. In tones that Griffiths would have approved of, I thundered 'Because if I stay in the Tanks ten years, I would never make an officer, *Sir*'. I then cautiously lowered my gaze and saw in descending order, snow white hair, a triple row of medal-ribbons and the blazing trews of a colonel of The Cameron Highlanders. The eyes seemed to show approval but Jehovah merely remarked 'I'll see what I can do, my boy'. Crash, crash, jump of inkwell, and I left with a small voice telling me that just for once perhaps I had said the right thing to the right man. I left Blackdown three days later with no regret except to wonder whether Bill Cody in the same troop ever got to the 11th Hussars. He opted for them giving a simple reason, that he 'liked the colour of their trousers', which were red and explained their 'Cherrypickers' nickname.

Back north I trundled, laden with full kit and became Officer Cadet C C Gunner at the Motor Battalion OCTU in the old Infantry Barracks, York. I was certainly at the Motor Battalion OCTU but, with fifty others, not really in it. The motor battalions were very much the property of those lordly regiments, the 60th and The Rifle Brigade, the Green Jackets. We were in the Support Wing to become machine-gun officers, and certainly not to entertain any foolish notions of bugle horns, black buttons or 140 paces to the minute.

Battle training in Tunisia; soldiers of 6th Royal Inniskilling Fusiliers (IWM)

The Green Jackets' cadets were a wonderful cross-section of the top ten public schools. I forget the ten which made up the approved list, except that Winchester was reputed to head Eton by a whisker, and that Rugby was a good furlong down the straight, but they were there, green felt cheesecutters firmly planted in the centre of the head, hair gently falling on to the jacket collar, hands in pockets and a kindly word for their old fags turning up on a new intake.

We were totally ignored: apartheid was never invented in South Africa. We even ate apart from the gods elected. Later I knew many of them in sterner conditions and liked them for their panache. Perhaps, apart from the Guards, they were the last link with 'ten to win and the last man in'.

Now it was back to square one for all of us. Those who arrived as sergeants, or even as did Rees, as a CSM of the Welsh Guards, were all reduced to that lowest of all ranks in the British Army, officer cadet. We were totally at the mercy of any lance-corporal on the staff, and always, twenty-four hours a day, faced the ultimate deterrent – RTU (returned to unit). As I never had a stripe this was no hardship for me, but others felt it keenly. It was recruit training all over again but with a refined difference. Now the object was not to turn out a soldier, it was to make one who had elected to become an officer crack and admit he was wrong.

Every device and skill was employed to that end. Goad him to say or do something and he was insubordinate and not officer material. If he did nothing and took it all, he was weak and not officer material either. Cadets had no rights at all and could never win. Punishment for everything was extra drill on Saturday afternoons and for five weeks my Saturdays were just that.

I achieved a Company record of ten extra drills when ordered on parade to turn out my small-pack to show that I was carrying the regulation mess-tins, socks, towel, and that mysterious friend, the 'housewife'. I displayed to an outraged Major Roberts, four pieces of stiffening and half a gas-cape ironed to a knife-like crease. As he shook this mutilated piece of Crown property, a forgotten bun, grown green with age, fell out and rolled slowly through the rear rank. I was a familiar figure to the extra drill sergeant, so much so that he once told me to take the parade for him with the shattering comment, 'because drill's all they say you are fit for'.

Life proceeded. We lugged the Vickers guns miles down Walmgate Stray, drilled and marched on the windy gravelled square, learned bicycle drill ('prepare to mount') in order to go swimming in York Baths and sat in icy Nissen huts for endless lectures. 'Wake Mister Lottenburg up please, Mister Smullen – thank you Mister Lottenburg – office at 1600 hours to see the Major.' A lot was crammed into those seventeen weeks, but I never did get to understand that damned dial sight. And all the time for the first ten weeks, the slow progress of disproving that idiotic reason you gave to the Army's wife-bashing question, 'Why do you wish to be an officer?'

I was deeply moved by one result of this system. While getting my kit ready one Saturday afternoon for the usual extra drill, I found I was alone in the barrack room save for Rees, late CSM, Welsh Guards. He was, of course, older than all of us, a peacetime regular and faultless as regards things military. Of late he had been the special target of a thoroughly nasty little swine – Sergeant Hamilton. Hamilton, a regular himself, hated all cadets, especially Rees. He knew Rees was his superior in every respect, and he knew what a trophy he would secure if Rees, of his own will, admitted he could not take it and asked to return to his regiment. To my discomfort, I saw Rees was sitting on his bed in tears. 'It's that bastard Hamilton. I can't stand any more, I'll see the major and go back to the Brigade. Christ, I was someone there. I took a crown off my sleeve to come to this fucking hole, a crown that took five bloody years to get – at least the Guards treat you like men. Fuck the bloody commission.'

Suddenly this was not a man older than myself, not an ex-CSM whom I secretly admired, not someone I always felt I should call 'Sir'. It was one of us, the down-trodden, ever-threatened No 1 Platoon. I too hated Hamilton for his spiteful ways and it was with the conviction of Marshall Hall at his best that I pointed out that that was just what Mister bloody Hamilton wanted – to get a CSM of the Household Brigade snivelling to an incredulous Major Roberts that he was beaten and wanted out. One of us, Smullen, Hill, Corbishley, Dunnett or Gunner, was nothing – that was routine stuff to get some jumped-up little bleeder to break – but a WO of the Guards – haha! The sneer on Hamilton's face would follow Rees all his life. I rose to some heights I fear, because I liked Rees, then looked at the clock and fled towards the square to receive my usual greeting: 'Nice to see you again Mister Gunner – now, get fell in.'

After OCTU, Rees and I only met once again, in a bar in Florence. He was a captain and had just won the MC – we both got very drunk, but never mentioned that day when we were alone in an empty barrack room.

Another favourite, if there was a favourite target, was Louis Lottenburg. A Jew from London in The Royal Fusiliers, Lotty could shave three times a day but would always be blue about the gills. He took it all without complaint, and had a bond in common with myself – he too had never had a stripe. We shared many an extra drill, but I think I just beat him to the record.

One day Lotty surprised Paddy Smullen and me by asking if we would go out to dinner with him at the Station Hotel. To go there was a rare treat at any time. It was for officers only, although cadets were tolerated, but it cost money and that was always the deterrent. He explained that his father was visiting the town and was taking him out for an hour if he could get away. He would like to take two friends; Dad would pay. That clinched it for Paddy and me. When Dad Lottenburg's Rolls Royce drew up outside the gates we all three scrambled aboard and ordered dinner at the Station as if we came there every night. We spoke of that dinner later, on an Italian hillside in 1944 when he visited me. He was then in the East Surreys and was killed the next day in village fighting north of Rome.

The end of OCTU drew near. We now wore a collar and tie, ate off a tablecloth, and Captain Gunnell, our platoon officer, was almost human. Some were sent away and three were 'back companied' to serve another five weeks. Lotty was one of the latter. I realised I would pass out after an interview with the Major, when he berated me with every failing from being dirty (Don't you take a bath, Gunner?) to bribing his batman to press my battledress.

They had won, the system had won, when I was stung to say, 'Yes, sir – but could I go out of here tonight and command a platoon of infantry?' – only to receive the cold answer 'Yes, and you would be bloody useless in barracks.' I made the mistake of allowing myself an insolent smile, a smile that earned me the comment 'And get that grin off your face, it's cost you an extra drill.'

The last day came and I was commissioned into The Royal Northumberland Fusiliers. In every locker was a best, London-made tunic with one pip glittering on each shoulder, a pair of gloves, a swagger cane, and that symbol of it all, a Sam Browne belt. For the last time we fell in as 'other ranks', for the last time we dressed by the right to the bellows and shrieks of the drill sergeants.

The band crashed into the National Anthem, and the Duke of Gloucester spoke to the man next to me. The Green Jackets roared past at the double – slings flapping and bugles screaming. We strode past to the majestic strains of *The British Grenadiers* under the patronising gaze of Eton and Jesus.

It was all over. Short of raping one of the NAAFI wenches, we had crossed the Great Divide. With an emotion that only Paddy Smullen of County Galway expressed, we put on that tunic and those gloves, and picked up that belt. Paddy paused for a moment. He took his tunic out of his locker, studied the star upon the epaulette, and said: 'Very good of King George to give me this'.

As we left to catch trains home, we passed the Company Office. On the veranda stood a solitary figure, the CSM. He saluted and greeted each of us as we passed.

*Soldiers of the Irish Brigade relaxing in a pool built by the Romans
at Heliopolis near Guelma after the North African campaign (IWM)*

Chapter 4

'To Afrikay'

The training is over and the young Second-Lieutenant Gunner is sent to Tunisia, where Allied Forces landed in November 1942 in an operation designed to meet Montgomery's Eighth Army and push the Germans and Italians out of Africa completely.

MORE QUICKLY than those who stayed and trained for D Day a year later, I was packed off to war.

After an unhappy few weeks with some incredible battalion of The Cheshires at Trearddur Bay in Wales, I found myself in Dorchester where the 1st Kensingtons were forming up for overseas. To my delight, I found Paddy Smullen again, and most unbelievable of all, many of the young squires from the Green Jackets. The battalion was mainly London-raised, a Territorial Army battalion of The Middlesex Regiment. After the utter chaos of drawing stores, having jabs, and losing pay books, the unit was finally landed at Liverpool docks alongside the *Samaria*, a 20,000 ton Cunarder. I knew none of the men at all, and very few of the officers, but my heart warmed to Corporal Flint, who, as we pulled out into the Mersey, confided in me that he had relieved a sleeping sapper of his kit as he, Flint, having experienced several false alarms before, had arrived unloaded, unbelieving and light-hearted until he was actually on the gangplank.

I was glad he was in our Company. We went up to Greenock where the convoy formed up, then left one day and, clearing the Tail of the Bank, headed towards the setting sun. Paddy practically ordered me to watch Donegal fade from sight. Two days out we all realised that troopships, even Cunarders, were not the ideal form of travel. I defy anyone who spent more than forty-eight hours aboard one ever to forget the stench of vomit, sweat, burnt paint and fumes on H deck, when blacked out for the night. We were lucky to be going the short way, and not the endless voyage to the Cape and beyond.

Incidents were few and the food magnificent, for the officers anyway. Distant booms we assumed were the destroyers dropping depth-charges on U-boats. Rumours never ceased circulating, crown and anchor never ceased operating. (Was it not illegal in the forces? I never found out the answer.) Roy Farran of SAS fame was a passenger and he spoke to me at lunch once. 'Pass the salt, please'. His MC and Bar, and three cavalry pips brought the salt to his plate in a blur. I would have poured it for him had he asked. John Tizer, of the Green Jackets, showed his qualities early. With a splendid disdain for notices which clearly stated 'No personnel allowed on or near the Bridge', he was spotted by the OC Troops not only on the bridge, but chatting with the Captain. When hauled in front of 'John Gilpin', the ship's adjutant, and asked what in hell he thought he was doing, he replied with a puzzled smile that he 'thought the Captain would appreciate a word with the son of one of the directors of the Line'. John Gilpin dismissed him with a warning, knowing in his heart that he was probably right.

A hospital ship passed at night, lit up like a cinema. We watched it almost in silence as it faded in a glow over the horizon. Would the men of 1914–18 have muttered 'lucky devils?' We did not.

Eventually, after passing through the Straits of Gibraltar at night, with sirens booming and a Spanish fishing-boat overturning in the bow wave, we awoke with Africa on the right. I am always thankful that I sought the deck as dawn broke, and saw the endless range of the High Atlas mountains between the sea and the clouds.

We went straight into Algiers, docked and then disembarked with great haste as the harbour was visited nightly by German bombers.

The march out began eastwards, but after some ten miles, a combination of sun and troopship conditions had taken their toll. Sergeants and officers were carrying two or three rifles each, and water bottles were in constant use. Once I was startled by a huge American GMC truck pulling up alongside myself at the back of the Company. A vast black face leaned out of the cab and with the comment, 'Mah, mah, you looks hot', handed me a tin of orange juice – a touch of southern comfort.

We reached Rouiba, some twenty miles from Algiers, at nightfall and there on La Ferme Melia, we stayed three weeks. The days were spent route marching in the blazing heat and perpetual dust. We marched to the coast daily and bathed at Ain Taya, then marched back. We were hot, sticky and a bit smelly when we got home, but it hardened us up again after the voyage.

More important, I began to know 7 Platoon. Names became faces, and I dutifully filled pages of the message book with 'next of kin; occupation; service'. After the initial stare of mutual suspicion Sergeant Johnny Bowley and I began a comradeship which lasted as long as we wore khaki, and lasts to this day, I hope. Where are you now, Johnny, with your cock-sparrow wit and impudence? You little living repository of all that is best in the London soldier! Think of me sometimes as you cross Putney Bridge. Many were Territorials, some Militiamen, most were Londoners. Some were clerks, labourers, bricklayers, even barrow-boys. My batman, John Howard, was the platoon wit and I never tired of his tales of Euston Station where he had been a porter. We were the same age, but he knew more of the world than I did. We had our intellectual, complete with curved pipe and glasses, we had the inevitable dirty little bastard who needed, and got, a chasing. We even had the 'old sweat' Corporal Boyce who, on marches, drove us mad with yarns of Barrackpore, Umballa, and the Afridis. I loved his stories, but they always ended with descriptions of 'chatty pots' full of clear water, cooling in the evening breezes of the Himalayas, and I was hot and thirsty at the time.

Jack Taff, 'Tiny' Waters, Jimmy Thorpe, 'Bunny' Williams, Kinner, Willets, Eaton, Ivy, Horton, Clewly, Carter, Boswell, most from the city, some from the Plough. How right the Great Corsican was – 'No bad soldiers, only bad officers.' Perhaps you deserved better at the head of our little world, six carriers, four Vickers guns and thirty men.

M Melia and his family were kind to us, and sometimes we had dinner with them. Monsieur, Madame, Lucette, Suzette, Alette, all *'pied noir'* now but then plying us with chocolate liqueur and tales of the 'Gentil Capitaine' of the Para who came there first. I grew to dislike his confident smile in the always produced photograph. I also resented Lucette, all of twenty, addressing me as 'M'sieur Le Bébé', and thought of growing a moustache.

There I acquired my liking for strong waters, a liking I have never lost, which has always been a comfort, often a joy and sometimes, I fear, a bloody affliction to my friends. Dining in Rouiba one evening with David Davidson, I followed up the vin ordinaire (two bottles each) with banana liqueur, which seemed very pleasant with the coffee. Outside in the street Thor's hammer split my skull, and I arrived back at the billet unconscious on a pile of water melons in an Arab donkey cart. Always drink banana liqueur with a trusty friend.

News came that the battalion was allocated to the 78th Infantry Division as support battalion and that my Company was to join The Irish Brigade. The Division was far away in Tunisia, resting and refitting after heavy losses in the Tunisian campaign, when we set off on the long journey to join them.

Lifted on tank-transporters (two carriers to each) we took the inland route via Medjez, Constantine, Souk Ahras, over the old battlefields. Perhaps this was a deep-thinking staff officer's gentle way of letting the new boys get some idea of what lay ahead. We rode and lived on the transporters, sleeping beside them when they halted. We had no eyes for the towering djebels or rocky valleys, although I noticed the profusion of poppies in the coarse grasses.

Even the gorge of Constantine with the breath-taking hairpin descent to the plain below, merely caused caustic enquiries as to the driver's abilities and the state of his brakes, and some movement to the side away from the vertical drop. We had eyes now only for war's junkyard, and slowly became aware of a new smell, one we did not know before; a cloying, sickly-sweet and unforgettable smell; the smell of death. Burnt-out tanks, four on one crest, shattered transport, old dumps of shells, and mortar bombs, strange signs to 'Lazarette' and 'Kampf Gruppe Witzig', abandoned artillery pieces and tin plates, with skull and cross-bones, clanking in the wind on strands of wire. How very quickly the words 'Achtung Minen' were understood by all. No translation was ever called for. I returned from one halt with my first trophy, a Bersagliere helmet, complete with cock feathers, which I mounted on a bracket of my carrier. I fired an abandoned Italian carbine and, to the joy of my crew, landed on my arse with the recoil. I was tempted to try a Red Devil hand grenade, but wisely desisted. Two weeks later some officer braver than I tried it and was killed as it exploded in his hand. We were still booby-trap conscious, which perhaps was as well.

One evening at sunset, we laagered outside Medjez el Bab and after a supper of fried bully and wild tomatoes, Paddy and I walked down the road to the shattered remains of the village. The road ran near to the river where the Hampshires had battled on its banks and in its shallows. Bullfrogs, of a size that would not have disgraced Toad Hall, bellowed in the reeds and slime, and I was convinced a body still lay on the far bank. At the entrance to Medjez was a very plain sign 'Keep out – Typhus'. We stayed only to note some troops of the French Algerian Corps, presumably typhus-proof, who seemed to be billeted in a smashed house, and also to register more strongly than ever, the smell that has been described ad nauseam.

It was pleasant to return to a bedroll under the transporter and to know that Howard would wake me at dawn with a mug of tea to which I would add a generous whiskey. Our first NAAFI allowance, of a bottle per officer, per week, at 8 shillings (40p) a bottle, was now arriving. Phillipville, where we slept on beds in an agricultural school, was not, alas, the famous girls' school with the notice 'Should you require a mistress in the night, press the bell', over each bed. El Hamma, Sousse and, at last, our camp at Hammamet. Now we met up with the real soldiers; regiments whose carriers had the names of battles painted on them, 'Djebel Ang', 'Tanngoucha', 'Le Kefs', 'Bou Arada' and men who seemed so very different and apart. They had been in battle – we had not. They seemed to regard our bungling enthusiasm with an amused contempt.

When ordered to report to the Faughs for some piffling exercise, I blush to think that I invaded their Mess tent, the very picture of an Aldershot warrior, complete with pack, map case, Verey light, pistol etc, to be greeted by the few, thank God, officers having tea. I was actually wearing a steel helmet and saluted an amazed Major Garret, who soon sent me packing.

In the hills of Grombalia we were trotting along at the double one day, when I was called over to a jeep where kindly Brigadier Nelson Russell enquired my name and dismissed me with 'Right, run on laddie', whilst his driver, a superior looking captain with an MC stared at me with cold distaste. I ran on, and during that night, began my hate relationship with mules and wadis.

Still, I suppose we were trying and soon Monty came to welcome us to *his* Eighth Army. Every unit knew the form by then. 'Break ranks, gather round. I've come to see you and you can see me. Are you getting enough beer (laughter)?' But the magic was new to us and it worked, although my clearest memory was that he had the Warwickshire Antelope tattoed on his forearm. I hope I am right, my Lord Field Marshal! Later, he summoned all the officers of the Division to a gigantic awning on the beach where he outlined the coming invasion of Sicily. Alone on his little dais with blackboard and fly whisk (we will now have a break for coughing), he discoursed, while lieutenant-generals squatted in the sand at his feet.

Arnold of Rugby could not have bettered it. We bathed, route marched, got sunstroke, got lost on the mudflats, inspected empty boots for scorpions, issued mepacrine, and wondered. I was sent with a party one day to the theatre at Sousse, to see Will Fyffe. I saw and heard him, which was more than some hard-looking cases in the Highland Division did. When he broke into *Rolling up the Clyde,* many of them could be seen to have something rolling down their cheeks. Carriers were waterproofed, kit checked, ammo loaded up and a gorgeous James Bond escape outfit issued to officers. My third fly button pointed north if balanced on a pin. Did we have a file in case of Colditz? I forget, but the silk map made a wonderful neck cloth. On our last evening, everyone went to the beach for a swim. Every battalion seemed to be there, and I paid no attention when screams came from nearby groups. Trodden on a rock, I thought, until something like a whip hit me on the arm. I squealed with surprise and pain, and joined the rush ashore. One late lingerer got it smack on his chatsbies and passed out. Routed by a swarm of minute jellyfish – an evil omen.

Later we moved to the docks where an LST (landing ship; tank) loaded our carriers up the ramp. A bearded and mad naval lieutenant seemed to be all the crew it had. He did everything, literally, including hauling up the ramp and squashing badly loaded carriers into the hold by main force. Then he delivered a flow of invective at someone in a launch who had ordered him to tow a beach mat behind his vessel. This was eventually attached and, as darkness fell, we put to sea, safe in the arms of whichever saint is detailed to look after mad sailors and floating mats.

*Officers of Irish Brigade Headquarters: Front row (L to R):– Capt R L Lowry
[now Lord Lowry]; Major M F Douglas-Pennant; Brigadier Nelson Russell,
commander of the Irish Brigade; Capt R M C Cunningham; Capt J F Griffith:
Back row (L to R):– Capt G K Parsons; Lieut L D Room; Capt P L Chalk;
Lieut W J Concannon; Lieut H N D Seymour; Lieut J E Harrison (IWM)*

Chapter 5

The Invasion of Sicily

On July 10th, 1943 Allied troops invaded Sicily. At first 78th Division was kept in reserve in Africa but two weeks later it was committed to the short Sicilian campaign.

THE VOYAGE took nearly two days, and I shared a little cubby-hole with a war correspondent, Captain Baldwin, who was not only well informed about great matters but pointed out to me that we were passing Malta. As it was midnight, this was not much help but he meant well. Look-out was kept for the Airborne Division; not aloft, as they drove Pegasus through the skies to do battle, but in the drink. Due to misfortunes and errors many of them, if lucky, were clinging to ditched gliders and hoping to be picked up. I believe many were, and certainly during the battles in Sicily we found many of them turning up in odd places where they had landed. Very useful additions they were too, for those who found them.

We beached at Syracuse, and invaded the soft underbelly without getting our feet wet. The Division was in a follow-up rôle after the assault divisions had gone in. They had certainly gone in a long way we thought, as we took the road to Floridia, Vizzini and Mineo, passing through dusty olive groves and filthy villages that smelt of spilt vino. Perhaps it was all over. Then, on the second night, far ahead, we saw a sight that held every eye, the faint blue-white flicker and flash of the guns, and very, very faintly, a distant rumble.

There it was at last, there was what it all meant. They were not firing on targets at Larkhill, not simulating some battle exercise on Salisbury Plain, not even trying to hit a Dornier over the Mersey. They were firing at German troops who soon would fire back at us. It became all too familiar, and later I slept and slept well many times, not only in the light of the muzzle flashes, but under the steel sheet wailing overhead. But that first view stayed with us forever.

The next night it was nearer and the outline of the hills could be seen in the flashes; the rumble became percussive.

One brigade was already in action attacking Catenanuova and next day, with Etna as the backdrop, I looked over the valley to where Centuripe crowned a mountain.

It was Snow White's castle on a peak, and looked beautiful, but the shell bursts were already creeping up the slopes and bursting on the village. Into the valley we plunged and I led 7 Platoon up the wrong track. Troops in nearby ditches were not wearing our sign, and a Canadian sergeant who did not seem very anxious to come on the road to assist me with the map informed me at the top of his voice that I was in their 'Goddam reserve company lines'. As I digested this and my driver sucked his teeth in resignation, a loud whistle and crash caused much ploughed land on my left to jump skywards.

Some Argus up ahead had taken me for the tip of an armoured division and meant to blunt it. Hasty revving and reversing took us back and my status as a navigator went to zero. Meanwhile, by what was called a 'great feat of arms' the Irish had stormed Centuripe with a Light Brigade charge, head up on the mountain, and got away with it.

So up to Centuripe we went, on the zig-zag track, to assist in consolidation. On the way up, the first lonely figures were seen at the roadside with a blanket thrown over the face. In the smashed and burning village square, any musings on eternity were soon dispelled by a very efficient and terrifying figure in a coloured dress-cap who ordered me to get on and join the company ahead pushing down to the river. This was Brian Clark, Adjutant of the Faughs.

From that moment, he was the 'thread of scarlet' that ran through my war. Adjutants, good adjutants, are regarded with respect, fear and occasionally hatred by subordinates. He was accorded all those emotions in full measure by all who knew him. He would have resented any other reaction and when I say he was a great soldier, that is the compliment he would value most.

I got my platoon down by the river that day without loss, after a German 88 had used us as ducks in a shooting gallery. Next day, with a barrage roaring overhead, we set up shop and sprayed the countryside with belt after belt of machine-gun fire. It was all very exciting as the Faughs and Rifles surged across the river Salso and we raised our sights to the cornfields beyond. Somehow I felt a bugler should have sounded the charge, but amid the hundred little acts of bravery spread before my eyes, I lifted my cap to the lone German sniper who, at long range, and in the middle of the barrage, plugged away at my Vickers until he exploded a round in the belt feeding 'Tiny' Waters' No 3 gun. That massive product of Wapping docks exploded with rage and ordered his No 2 to fit a new belt, under pain of having his 'chest kicked in'.

Now it was time to dismantle the stall, climb on the carriers, and get up to the leading companies. The Sappers, those labourers of battle so often killed, spanner in hand, and always lacking a minstrel, had already put a rough crossing in the shallows. Leaving the platoon on the road I crossed on a motorbike for more orders from him 'who wore the coloured hat'. These were brief and simple, 'Get up here at once', here being where he and Colonel Butler now sat behind a cactus hedge with the leading companies.

Just then a burst of Spandau fire hit the hedge and killed an artillery signaller. I returned down the road at TT speed, which did not deceive the Germans who put me and my bike in the ditch with a dud shell. It was then I found disaster had struck. A heavy concentration had hit the platoon and Sergeant Williams and Corporal Kinner lay dead and Willets, Eaton, Howard and Horton were wounded. I was stunned. In a daze and assisted by the Padre of the Skins, we got the wounded away, and the two dead men off the road.

I remembered enough to remove their paybooks and identity discs, but when later in the day the same Padre said the burial service over two slit trenches, and crosses of broken boxes, I could not remember their numbers or initials.

The reserve platoon went up to do our job ahead as evening fell, and their officer, the monocled, stately Scot, De Pinna, delivered the last thunderbolt of the baptism of the battle. Paddy Smullen was dead. Back over the river he had been killed instantly by a shellburst. With the platoon dug in by the carriers and in the dark, I wandered away and there, under an olive tree, I sobbed my heart out.

A natural reaction to tension a psychiatrist may say, but it was plain grief at the loss of Williams and Kinner and the knowledge that never again would Paddy sit in the sunlight with *Ulysses* open on his lap. About midnight I was visited by my company commander, Captain Teddy Cullen, who had called with a double purpose. One was to ask me to pay up the money I had collected for the Naafi issue a week before, and secondly, to order me to carry up rations to the forward platoon on the next river. I pointed out that balancing his accounts at two in the morning in a place still being shelled, and where none dared show a light, was plain damn stupid, and he could go to hell with his Naafi. Ever pugnacious, he took issue with me, but his good nature could not keep it up and he departed agreeing that another time would do, leaving me with dixies and tins to lug forward.

Between the forward platoon and my ration party were olive groves, cornfields and a railway embankment. Mindful of some tactical lecture of the past, I lined up my band on the railway and at a word we all sprinted over the crest together – dixies, tins and weapons jingling like a smithy. Down the far slope we crashed into the forward platoon's carrier park. The sight and sound of this sudden charge from the rear was too much for the lonely sentry left on guard. He assumed the worst and surrendered to us.

Next morning the little town of Adrano in front was ground to dust by continuous flights of medium bombers and gunfire.

The Faughs were across the river and just short of the town and during the day's action, Tom Cammiade was wounded and picked up by the Hermann Goering Division. He was left behind when they pulled back at dusk, and retaken by his own battalion. Before the Germans left him a souvenir specialist relieved him of his wrist watch. Many months later, Tom returned to the Brigade, and at an inspection one morning recognised his own watch on the wrist of a rifleman. On asking how the watch had come to the rifleman, he received the amazing reply, 'Sure I took it off a dead German in Sicily, sir'. After some bargaining, Tom bought back his own watch for £5.

Adrano, Bronte and Randazzo fell, and with the link up with the Americans, the Sicily show was over. We lived under canvas on the lava-strewn slopes of Etna, in solitude and peace. Malaria struck the Division, causing more to succumb than the battle casualties. One morning, I delivered eight of my platoon to the Casualty Clearing Station and saw, in tents and lying in the open, about two hundred cases. To get away from this pest house the entire Division was moved down to the coast at Falcone and Patti.

The move was unforgettable for producing the biggest traffic cock-up, caused by the Highland Division, known to us as the Highway Decorators, as they never passed a building, gun or knocked-out enemy tank, without slapping their famous HD on it in blue paint. I believe they even put it up on Waterloo Station on their return to the UK. They justified that by claiming that 'Scots Regiments won Waterloo anyway'; they forgot how many of the men at Waterloo were Irish.

All day, in jerks and stops, we crawled to the seaside. Troops lay gasping under the vehicles at every halt, and the lucky owners of German Trinkwasser containers, doled out the nectar.

It was August and very, very hot. Grapes as large as plums hung in places, but not for long. Howard did get one bunch before the rush and gave me a few. It was when the convoy seemed to get unstuck and started to motor down to the Sea of Sicily, that we passed the most beautiful girl I ever saw, standing at the door of a farm, watching the soldiers go by. About seventeen, barefoot, ragged black skirt and black jersey, she stood with some old women, completely unaware of her beauty, and the effect it produced. Lorries, tanks, jeeps, artillery, all paused and gaped. Taking my cue from a major-general who stopped his jeep for a look, I too halted my carrier until irate shouts from behind moved us on. She was the eternal Paesani of those barren rocks, watching Saracens, Crusaders, Teutons, Lombards or French, filing past. No doubt she would have produced the same effect on them, and no doubt she will be gazing there still when the name of Montgomery is as distant and remote as John of Gaunt.

Our little holiday by the sea was only marred by the results of too many grapes, too much bathing and as much vino as could be bought, bartered or looted. The latrine poles had to be reinforced to cope with the customers and even Biscuit Burgoo did not have the cementing effect claimed by the Medical Officer.

All the battalion officers dined together one night in a tent overlooking the shore and I was detailed as Mister Vice. That merely means sitting at one end of the table opposite the Mess President, and at his call 'Mister Vice, the King,' rising glass in hand to say 'Gentlemen, the King'. It is no distinction and falls to all junior officers in turn. Perhaps it was the special Marsala that we had that night, perhaps it was the thought of, even better, the Irish Whiskey to follow, but looking down the candlelit table past Teddy Cullen's shoulder, I could see the white line of the surf, the moon track on the water, and those unblurred and touchable stars of the inland sea. As I rose to the toast, I thought that it was a fine place and time to honour the Sovereign who had given Paddy that star which had shone so briefly on his shoulder.

*The pipes of The Royal Irish Fusiliers beat retreat and play traditional Irish airs
at a military hospital in Tunisia (IWM)*

Chapter 6

'Soft Underbelly . . .'

After Sicily the Allied armies moved into the Italian Peninsula. It was designed to be a thrust at the 'soft under-belly' of Europe. Instead it turned out to be a long and bloody slog up through Italy. Colin Gunner's company of the Kensingtons was very active in supporting the Irish Brigade and his admiration for the fighting Irish soldiers increased.

JON THE cartoonist once pictured the Two Types studying a newspaper in June 1944, and muttering 'D Day, D Day, which one do they mean, old boy?' Well, I was off on my second one now to Italy, and very pleasant it was too. The Salerno landing had gone in, and already grim rumours flew around of waiting Germans, heavy losses and hanging on with finger nails.

The Straits of Messina had exploded with a Monty barrage of hundreds of guns, but as it turned out, Brocks Fireworks Company would have done just as well as no opposition was encountered. But how one blessed that insurance policy that the old fox always had up his sleeve! Easy to sit with Clausewitz open before one and talk of 'risks; thrusting on; open flanks; brush them aside' and other Prince Rupert sentiments. I can only say that to the exasperated infantryman, already hot and weary after a night covered in dust, groping for the tapes that led him to the start line, and buggered about by last-minute changes from equally harassed officers, it was some comfort to hear the floodgates open behind him and see his objective tossing in a sea of shells, even if the last German had left hours before. I like to think it was some comfort also to those ghosts who always stood at Monty's elbow, ghosts from the Vimy Ridge, the Schwaben Redoubt, and Delville Wood. Some of their sons were in our midst.

But, as far as we were concerned, we were being sent off on a glorious happy-go-lucky, vino-swigging carnival of liberation. I took 7 Platoon to join a Jock column that sailed from Catania to Taranto. Like all Jock columns it was a hotch-potch of all arms – tanks of the County of London Yeomanry, guns, some armoured cars of the Recce Regiment, lorried infantry and three platoons of the Kensington machine-guns on carriers. To Taranto we sailed in LSTs and for the first time at sea I got a bunk to myself. The two previous times I had slept on a metal deck that vibrated and smelt of oil, so I felt things had started well.

27

As we entered the outer harbour with (it was said) an Italian pilot, a bang behind us in the column of ships turned out to be the minelayer *Abdiel* which had hit a mine that broke her back; she sank in minutes. As she was carrying many of the Para boys, already loaded up for disembarkation, losses were heavy. We went on into the inner harbour and passed several Italian submarines on the stocks before we grounded. As in Sicily no feet got wet and, armed with a *Michelin Guide to Italy*, we were told to push on towards Bari. I halted and harboured for the night by a deserted power station in the middle of nowhere. Amid silent turbines, echoing walls and acres of dials, I was welcomed by a jolly QM of the South Staffordshires airborne battalion. He was alone save for his batman and driver, but had with him the rum ration. Together with my platoon we made merry in those weird surroundings and I do not know to this day where I slept on my first night in Europe proper, but I certainly woke with the warmest regard for all wearers of the red beret. Not far from there their General Hopkinson was sniped and killed by some tough little rearguard of Germans. I seemed to have no orders and no-one in immediate command, so on we trundled to Bari. Now and again, we met some Paras in captured cars and lorries, but they all seemed to be on missions of their own. It wasn't until I met some Shermans of the Yeomanry and an artillery major that I felt we were not liberating Italy on our own. Down at Bari seafront I really got the hang of things; clapping and cheering crowds, bottles of vino handed to appreciative troops, Sergeant Johnny Bowley with a pretty girl on his carrier – and a kiss for me from an unshaven, rancid smelling old man.

My carriers were low on fuel and the rubber on the bogies was stripping off fast. Also no mention of rations had been made at Taranto and the boxes of compo packs we carried would not last for ever. I stopped at what turned out to be the Italian Air Force HQ, an imposing building on the corner, and demanded food, petrol and any transport that was available. Greeted and welcomed by a delightful Italian Air Force captain in Savile Row dove grey, I was taken up to the fourth floor to Il Generale, a charming man with white hair. For the first time I heard the litany that was to follow us until the day we crossed the Alps into Austria: 'Tedeschi rubari galline, maiale, uoa, vino, benzina tutto tutto tutto'. The Germans had taken everything.

This was true in most cases and as always, the blow fell heaviest on the poorest villagers. But at that time pity for the Italians did not fill our hearts. In the end I managed to get bread and a motorbike which Jimmy Thorpe, the DR, viewed with contempt. After Bari, village followed village, river followed river, some by day in blazing sunshine, some by night amid bonfires, cheers and barking dogs. Only flashes and flickers like the spurts of a dying fire stand out such as the night amid shrieks and kisses, lit by the flames of the Mayor's house when I was assured that the Germans were just leaving by the corner of the church. Rifle in hand, followed by a throng that dwindled to one small boy, I set off to liberate my personal corner of Europe.

Certainly something crashed away in the vineyard, followed by my random bullets and I probably scared the hell out of the priest's donkey, but it went down well and I graciously accepted many cognacs before pushing on. The platoon with their usual good sense had accepted more than me as they waited for the little war to end, and I had to speak sharply if thickly to Private Carter before his carrier joined the weaving waving column to head north. That night I spotted a belligerent youth waving a Colt automatic and, despite his sobs of protest, I added it to my armoury.

Then there are the other memories: the disillusion of the owner of the fish shop as we brewed up on his stock of boxes; the fawning servility to an officer's stars of a frightened padrone in the big house, and his amazement when informed that the soldiers did indeed share the billet with the officer and he had better make room for them bloody subito; the look on Private Abrahams' face, dug in on a riverbank, when I informed him that he was the right hand man of the Eighth Army; the grand moment when the Column commander appeared in a jeep and shouted to me 'On to Bitonto' (the next village), a gesture worthy of 'Blood and Guts' himself and only spoiled by his roaring on alone and pausing to ask a German sentry the way; whilst his jeep did the proverbial turn on a sixpence, the aggrieved German dived into a house to fetch his fowling-piece which he discharged at a cloud of dust; the morning when our Recce armoured car saw a lorry-load of the opposition turn out of a side road and carry on in the same direction as them; with some quick thinking the sergeant of the armoured car removed his green beret and closed until his gun was almost over the Germans' tailboard. Then, still waving cheerily and giving the passengers a friendly thumbs-up, he fired; I passed the blazing corpse-strewn wreck ten minutes later and changed my opinion of the much derided two-pounder gun; at a range of ten feet, loaded with HE, it is effective.

The cry now was Foggia. The objective, we were told, was to secure the airfields, said to be the biggest in Italy. Michelin marked Foggia but where in hell the airfields were was anyone's guess. At 10 that night, 7 Platoon was across a good road and secure for the night. A visit by Teddy Cullen earlier with some welcome rations had told me that we were near to the goal. Warning my forward gun positions, I set off alone in the olive groves keeping the road on my left. After a while, the groves stopped. Kneeling down, I could see in the starlight a very large flat plain ahead. Without knowing it, I was on the edge of the airfields. I returned to the roadside and was rolled up in the blanket when the sound of engines woke me. A jeep, followed by some twenty more, was stopped by Sergeant Bowley and I saw an amazing collection of armed bandits sitting on and in them. Their leader, to whom I spoke, looked like Lord Byron, and the conversation ran thus: 'Who are you?' 'Popski's Private Army, old boy – just going into Foggia to have a look'. 'Well, there's a great flat field in front and we're the last troops on this road as far as I know'. 'Thanks old boy, we'll be off – oh, by the way, don't open up if we come back in a hurry – goodnight'. They chugged past, dripping with K guns, automatics, and grenades; dressed in the rejects from Harrods' spring sale, cap comforters, Italian helmets, jumping jackets, scarves and desert boots. A top hat would not have surprised me. As they disappeared Johnny Bowley remarked admiringly, 'What a shower'. Well, the 'shower' got into Foggia and next morning ambushed a German convoy with great efficiency. They also left a great impression on 7 Platoon who later had to be prevented from copying their sartorial tastes.

An 88 mm gun crew stopped the lot at Serracapriola and the Northants debussed a company to take the village. As we followed them up I found a woodcutter's hut containing a German's breakfast on the table and, joy of joys, a German parachutist's jumping jacket.

Jimmy Thorpe and I shared the breakfast, but that jacket was mine. Embellished later with a fleece lining, and a fur collar, I felt every inch a Field Marshal in it, although I never dared to wear it in the forward positions in case of mistaken identity.

As the Northants got near the village a sound like a football crowd broke out and white sheets appeared at every window. Climbing up the steep path to the usual reception, we saw the 88 abandoned and all the crew dead around it. The inhabitants of Serracapriola had timed their blow at their late ally to the second and by the look of the bodies had opened up with muskets loaded with bicycle chains.

We joined the Northants in the square and I took my own carrier on to the end of the village. Propped against the wall I saw what I took to be one of the Northants' wounded. A closer look as I went up to him made me jump. He was a sergeant-major of the German army and badly hurt. A shell had hit the wall behind him splattering his back with shrapnel but after a drink from my water bottle, which never contained water, he stood up and we helped him into the carrier. He was a big chap and in pain but holding on to the sides he kept his feet until we got to the stretcher post in the square. There, flushed with their victory, the crowd of Italians surged forward with cries of vengeance. I helped him out and as he stood up by the side of the carrier he snarled one word, *Schweinhund*, and with a backhander belted the nearest two across the face. It was Horatius on the Bridge – 'as lo the ranks divide' – and I helped him to the stretcher post in silence from the mob. I shall always be proud to remember that never once did I see in the front line an unkindness to a German prisoner. The old Eighth Army had many faults: thank God that was not one of them. As I got him there I was in time to hear the Northants CSM tell two grubby-looking civilians to get the hell away from his Company HQ, only to be told by one of them, in those inimitable accents, that he should not address officers of the Coldstream Guards in that fashion and that they would like a word with the Company commander. And Guards officers they were too, the first of many escaped prisoners we picked up along the road later.

Next morning should have warned us, as the Luftwaffe appeared and dive-bombed the village burning many vehicles which had been crowded in. As we had passed on some two miles by then we could sit on a hillside and take a detached view of it all. That was until, from nowhere, three Spitfires dived down and, in less than thirty seconds, columns of smoke marked the end of three Focke Wulfs. A mad dash down the hillside ensued, led by me brandishing a machete, to cut the souvenirs from the wrecks, only to find a black and blazing crater. Unknown to us as wc followed our carnival career, 36 Brigade plus a Marine Commando was on the Termoli bridge ahead, having taken another route and it was this ridge that we studied across a wide valley the following morning. With an artillery observer, I sat on a bank and sensed that something was going on up on that ridge, something big. Much noise could be heard and black columns of smoke were shooting up near the town. I called up Corporal Ivy with his rangefinder to get a better look. A Panzer Division (the 16th) had been pulled out of the Salerno area and, having travelled across Italy by night, was now attacking 36 Brigade with all their old ferocity. It was like watching a panorama of toy soldiers. Tanks motored up, paused, and with a puff of flame, fired. Lorries followed them and German infantry debussed in drill style, formed up and, shaking out into line, moved forward.

They were out of range of our Vickers guns, but the artillery officer called for fire from his battery far behind us. This too fell short but then, much nearer and at the foot of the ridge, five Mark IVs led by a motorcyclist, came round the bend in the road. They paused and I could see the leading tank commander leaning out of his turret talking to the motorcyclist. Without hesitation the artillery officer called a correction and after whistling high above us I saw the shell burst only yards from the lead tank. The reaction was instantaneous. The turret lid slammed shut and in his haste to back off round the corner he squashed the motorbike under his tracks. By now all the platoon were up and jostling for a look through Ivy's instrument and whilst thus engaged, were scattered by Teddy Cullen, now all heavy business, ordering everyone to get on the move. He took me to one side and briefly told me that 36 Brigade was being wiped out. The Irish Brigade was coming up by sea to try to hold Termoli and we were to get there at top speed. The impresario departed. The carnival was over. Even the weather changed, as in drenching rain we moved off towards the black columns of smoke and the muttering gunfire. Jack Tuff, my driver, hung his steel helmet on the gear stick and threw an empty vino bottle over the side.

Chapter 7

The Longest Night

In early October 1943 the Irish Brigade were shipped from Barletta along the eastern coast of Italy to Termoli. They arrived in the midst of a vicious battle for the town which had been attacked by the German 16th Panzer Division. The Termoli battle was the first of a series of actions for the Brigade on that side of Italy.

THE IRISH Brigade filtered into Termoli or that part that was still held during the day. Some came by the road; most came by sea. The Faughs arrived in a Dunkirk style armada. They were greeted by fountains of water, in the middle of which a stout-hearted commando sergeant in a rowing-boat could be heard asking to speak to the colonel. This he did, and thanks to this brave man, Colonel Butler had a picture of the situation, albeit a gloomy one, before he landed.

The escorting destroyers put on their famous impression of the ocean greyhound and fired broadsides inland until a German tank whose crew had never heard of Nelson motored up to the cliff edge and planted some shells into one of them. Perhaps he was thinking of 'wooden walls' but as the navy, invoking the shade of Jack Fisher, formed a line of battle he smartly withdrew and no doubt radioed Berlin to claim the *Ark Royal*.

I joined up with the Faughs as they started the counter-attack. No time was lost as none was available. I was only told to tag on to their support company and, reporting to John McNally, their major, I waited with them as the rifle companies started along the ridge. The guns were going flat out now and I was somewhat depressed when Private Carter informed me with gloomy relish that our guns had been prepared for demolition in case the attack failed.

As we waited the black-haired and too good-looking Irishman, Sergeant Taylor, found time to rummage around in a large villa, said to be Count Ciano's and emerge with a magnificent silk table runner, embroidered with a coat of arms. This I believe enriches some room in Ireland to this day. The grin on his swarthy face as he showed me his trophy soon vanished as Major McNally ordered the company forward to the brickyard. The Faughs and Skins were clearing the way faster than had been hoped.

The brickyard, like all brickyards, had a tall chimney and that chimney was the aiming mark for every gun the Germans could bring to bear. It was no place to linger as they pumped shells into it. By it blazed one of the dreaded

German Tiger tanks, those unstoppable monsters; in and around it sprawled many dead Argylls and Germans. Among the Argylls lay a very great Scottish soldier, Major John Anderson, VC, DSO.

Little wars raged around the brickyard while the rifle companies battled a few hundred yards ahead. We were getting fire from our right where the valley sloped and I hope General Bredin, as he now is, will forgive me if I say that a vivid cameo of the brickyard battle was formed by his backside hanging over the bank as he fired burst after burst of Bren gun fire at the enemy.

Up ahead, two black columns shot up where one of the supporting Canadian tanks had brewed up two German Mark IVs. As these Canadians were from the Trois Rivières Regiment, this came over the air in French and some listening German must have got very confused wondering if de Gaulle had left London. The order to move came none too soon for Jimmy Thorpe the DR. I gave him up as lost when he came out of the brickyard and vanished in the smoke of a shellburst, but he shot out the other side with his brew-can still hanging from his saddle – all was well. On the objective at the end of the ridge I found Colonel Butler having a chat with his opposite number, the German commander. The colonel was his usual smiling and serene self, upright, stick in hand, whilst things whizzed through the air causing weaker souls to duck and blink. The German commander, a hauptmann (captain), was not so happy. He lay wounded in the ditch, while with him squatted his orderly. Quite calm and totally unhurt, a boy of about 18, the orderly had refused to leave his commander and had waited for us to take him prisoner. I hope that hauptmann remembers him as we remember him.

As the tanks milled around and order started to be imposed, nine Spitfires circled us, very low. They came, saw and didn't like what they saw, as going into line astern, they swooped down. Not until we saw open-mouthed, blue lights flickering along the wings of the leader did we believe it was happening.

Then the ditch turned into a layer cake. The Germans at the bottom, some of the reserve company, plus Brian Clark and his signallers formed the chocolate in the centre, then on top and horribly exposed the duller witted, comprising myself, various runners and hangers-on. The cake heaved and boiled as the strafing went on, plane by plane, and that German hauptmann must have been shouting something about the Geneva Convention but the only thought in my mind was to join him at the bottom. Brian Clark, however, is bigger than me and my burrowing only met a broad khaki back.

The Canadian tank major most gallantly stood on his turret waving a tricolor flag until, with the bullets hitting his tank, he slammed down his hatch with shrieks of 'Albion perfide'. The Spits then bombed us and we lost some men. Recriminations of these incidents were old hat even then, just as was a gun firing short in a barrage. They were a fact of life that infantry lived with. The layer cake came to life and the breathless and ungrateful Germans were helped out of their refuge. Colonel Butler was annoyed and this may have been why he gave Brian a sharp telling-off for being slow getting up to him.

It perhaps discomforted Brian, but it did the listening soldiers' morale a power of good to hear the Adjutant getting a rocket from the Colonel. I took my guns to Major Tommy Wood on the right of the ridge. This was the first time I had met that legendary figure of the Faughs. A survivor of all the battles of Africa and Sicily, the wearer of a dress cap and green scarf as he led his company into action, this was the man who tapped a Bren gunner on the head with his stick and ordered 'Kill those men' as standing upright he indicated a Spandau crew fifty yards away. He was that sheet anchor of the infantry, a great rifle company commander. Now he sat in the rain calling the roll with a blanket over his head, and notebook in hand. Lady Butler would not have painted the scene as in 'After the Charge', but it had a nobility that no crested helmets or pennoned lances could ever capture. As he had no officer I tried to make myself useful to him and after digging the guns in, we buried several Germans, including a lieutenant, in the gully.

I did not bury the lieutenant's mapcase, one of those superior leather ones, but transferred it from his belt to mine. The rain fell all that night and occasional crashes proved that the Germans had not retreated far. At dawn, we thought that they had gone a long way back as, cautiously at first, we explored around. I was amazed by one body in the plough that I found. It was Edmund Blunden's 'Death could not kneel thus', but he did kneel and was quite upright. He was one of our anti-tank gunners with a machine-gun burst in the stomach. I found a knocked-out Mark IV down the bank complete with dead crew and got the commander's Luger after a gruesome minute leaning into the turret. Better still, in a box, they had some of our property they had taken in their attack; two thousand Woodbines and five tins of treacle. Riches indeed, as I had paid ten shillings (50p) two days before for four Craven A to a bombardier of the artillery.

I then joined Major Wood who was sitting, field-glasses to his eyes, studying the front. I soon saw what fascinated him. About five hundred yards out in the valley a flock of geese milled around a farmhouse, honking and flapping happily. No orders were needed as he nodded towards them and remarked 'They don't seem to have an owner'. Here was my chance to shine in the eyes of my hero so, gathering up three of my platoon, I set off on my goose chase. Disillusion was awaiting me. Going to the farm I adopted what I thought to be a cunning approach, along a hedge with a convenient ditch. I

*Officers of the Faughs: the front row includes (from L) Capt R L G Wood; Capt
B D H Clark; Major H G G Garrat; Major H Rogers (2nd i/c) Lt Col B H Butler
(CO); Capt R C P Jefferies (Adjutant); Major R M Cunningham; Capt P J Proctor
and Lt E Maginness (QM). Also included are Major Jimmy Clarke (fourth from L
in back row) and Lt Hunter Lang, Medical Officer (on R of middle row) (IWM)*

thought Tommy would appreciate such soldierly precautions and also I thought of a waiting German sniper anxious to put a Mauser bullet into the goose-hunter.

Halfway along the hedge a bellow from the ridge above froze me. 'Get up, you yellow bastard!' Turning, I saw him waving me on vigorously. Up I got and marched to the farm. The ensuing slaughter was horrible, as most of it had to be done with shovels and claspknives, but eventually we puffed up the slope, smeared with blood and feathers, carrying enough geese to feed the Army. Tommy inspected Little Smithfield in the gully, and remarked 'Well done', so I was forgiven my timid attack on Goose Farm. Our little ridge had now become a bedlam of all arms. Even Mahrattas from the 8th Indian Division had come up for battle experience and Johhny Bowley brandished some of their tea under my nose with the comment, 'Look at it – different from that bloody dust they give us'. He was right, it was splendid tea and their chapaties were even better.

A battery of Long Toms had dug in behind us and they went too far as night fell. Fires sprang up and little groups relaxed around them with tea and song. Perhaps that was how they always behaved but to C Company of the Faughs, dug in only a few yards away on stand-to and forbidden to show a light, it seemed a bit too much. Murmurs arose but Tommy only said contemptuously that a few shells on them would soon quieten them down. The trouble was that the shells would fall on us as well.

So I summoned the chap who had surrendered to his own side in Sicily, a soldier not renowned for his military ardour, but a cheerful and willing little comedian. We rigged him up in my German jumping jacket, took a German helmet from a grave and put it on his head and thrust two German stick grenades into his (German) belt. He now looked the very picture of a stormtrooper, apart from his size. Then driving him with blows and curses we hustled him past the festive artillery. He played up well and kept squeaking 'Kamerad – achtung – Heil Hitler' or whatever German he knew.

Johnny Bowley, the stage manager, explained to the horrified spectators that we had 'caught the bastard creeping up the slope – and he says there's more of the sods with him'. Never did night fall more swiftly. Fires vanished with a hiss, songs died away, safety catches clicked off for miles, officers radioed for help and grabbed for rusted revolvers. Out of sight, the 'stormtrooper' was restored to the British Army and returned to sleep soundly with the rest of us.

Battle patrols reported that the way ahead over the valley was clear. More than that, they reported an intact bridge over the River Trigno. Bridges, intact bridges, must have had some dreadful fascination for the planners at GHQ; at our level we could not fathom why this should be so. We never saw one intact all the time we fought in Italy, save in Rome and Florence, and indeed the surest indication of any enemy withdrawal was to watch the glow at night as they blew up the bridges, but still the fascination persisted. Was there a jackpot prize reserved for bridge-capturing generals? Would such a general, in years to come, be able to stride into the Cavalry Club amid awed murmurs of 'He's the chap who got a bridge'? We never knew, but as we formed up at nightfall to seek that elusive prize, Dicky Hodsell surprised me by asking 'Have you got a tin hat?' On my assuring him that it was on my carrier he spoke the words of prophesy 'Because by God you'll need one tonight.'

He was dreadfully correct, but one night out in his prediction. As per the drillbook the bridge rose skywards as Tommy Wood and his company set foot on it.

It was also heavily mined and booby-trapped and some twenty casualties resulted, mostly from those horrors full of ball-bearings that jumped in the air and exploded. We got going in the dark, but did not get to the bridge until dawn was breaking. I got the platoon and carriers into a gully off the road but we had been noted. As the last two carriers nosed off the road the old whistle and crash came down on us fair and square, and Private Smith was mortally wounded. To get him to the Aid Post meant going forward to the Faughs BHQ near the bridge, but the road was out of the question now. So at the best speed we could, we took the stretcher over the fields . No more shells fell and we reached Faughs BHQ safely but Smith was gone as I could see only too well when the gasping, sweating stretcher-bearers laid him down and Baker, the Faughs' Medical Sergeant, looked on without comment. More stuff flew over and with forebodings I saw it land in our gully again. Back over the fields we returned and again found that it had landed all too accurately. This time Johhny Howard, my batman, was down, but conscious. Amid several more salvoes, all smack on target, we got him on the stretcher and set off again during a lull. He spoke to me on the way and apologised for being 'so much trouble'. Dying and jolted on an already bloody stretcher *he apologised.* Before we reached BHQ he suddenly said 'It's getting dark Sir' and pulled the blanket over his own face. We saw instantly, as he had seen, that the end had come and he had made his own exit from this vale of tears unaided by us. His father, a 1914-18 soldier, moved me to tears when he wrote later and said that many times he had watched the rain on his window in London and wondered 'where the boys are digging in tonight.' Perhaps his family met their grief with the same dignity that Private John Howard met the darkness. All who laughed at his tales of Euston Station would hope so.

Colonel Butler with his unfailing kindness and urbanity now showed me where he wanted my machine-guns to be sited and as we returned to his HQ in the sunken lane, acknowledged a salute that did my shaken nerves a lot of good. The salute came from Dick Richards of the Faughs who paused from digging a slit-trench and gave his Colonel a parade-ground salute that Wellington Barracks could not have faulted. He was an ex-sergeant of the Skins, decorated and commissioned on the field in Africa and, as I found out later, when I served under him, if indeed I did not sense it then, a born leader.

Day faded, and as the companies splashed over the shallows to join the others in the bridgehead, the longest night began. I waited with S Company to cross the river when called. It was an early zero-hour, too early for everyone, but designed to give the attacking companies and the Rifles on the right all night to get clear of the wood that formed the bridgehead and forward onto the ridge ahead; then we would rattle over and join them in time for breakfast. But as the guns opened out and we clambered onto the carriers we saw a sight that made that breakfast seem a dream. German shell and mortarfire crashed into the wood until it twinkled with light; Spandau after Spandau opened up with their calico rip and red streams screeched into the flashing pandemonium. The shallow little Trigno had become the Styx and old Charon was busy with his boat. Waiting and out of touch we could only guess at the progress of any of the attack, but faces lengthened and rumours flew.

We did not know that all the leaders of the first wave were dead; that the companies had caught it on the startline; that nobody could get on and that great gaps were being torn in the battalion by the German fire; that Paddy Proctor, Dennis Dunn and Kevin O'Connor, men on whom would depend success or failure, were dead; that those iron rivets of the infantry, the company sergeant majors and platoon sergeants, were down or falling; that Corporal Wolf had seen a hayrick coming at him and knew too late that it was a German tank; that the Rifles were hit as hard as us and were taking heavy losses; and that finally the bright spirit of the attack had been extinguished and that Colonel Butler lay dead. With the wood crashing around him, with his beloved companies shattered, despite pleas to take cover, he met his end in the only way anyone could have envisaged; in the only way any infantry colonel could wish – erect, calm and very unafraid.

From somewhere we got orders to cross, and over the shallows and into the wood we went. Almost at once came orders to cross back again and with prayers that the fire would not shift on the ford we went back to the home side. Night was far advanced, although I privately was convinced that it would never end, when someone, God knows who, said that we must cross again. Once had been bad enough but a second time really caused some heaving of the bowels. I could not blame one of the gun numbers who risked

*During a lull in the Cassino battles two Faughs take
the opportunity to relax (IWM)*

being grilled on the engine-cover so that he could attain the totally horizontal, inside a Bren-carrier.

Before we had cleared the shallows and only the first two carriers were on the far bank, another voice in a darkness full of cries and crashes told us to go back. Whose voice it was I wonder now, but it was obeyed, but not before I saw in a sudden flash a body stark naked and the colour of a baked rabbit. My total contribution to the night was to load on my carrier, before re-crossing again, three stretcher-cases and as many walking wounded of the Faughs as I could get aboard. With one of them giving Jack Tuff, the driver, directions and myself trying to hold a stretcher steady on the back we heaved up out of the shallows and back on the road with a nameless major appearing who seemed to want everyone to go back across yet again! I had a vision of a court-martial for cowardice as I went on and delivered the casualties to a stretcher post before seeking the oft-quitted and oft-revisited sunken lane. I was too damned tired and jumpy to worry too much about him as explosions on the road prevented any more yo-yoing over rivers. Very wearily the platoon lined the lane and stuck the guns through the hedge overlooking that now silent and smoking wood. Day had come but no-one felt inclined to do much about it. Even the ritual of the brew-up was stilled

Johnny Bowley, his fountain no longer bubbling and sparkling, sat silent beside his carrier. I lit a cigarette and silently handed one each to Jack Tuff and Abrahams. A figure approached down the lane with a familiar swagger. Tommy Wood strode up, dress-cap and polished regimental badge, brass crowns on shoulder, and revolver on his belt. A map-case flapped at his side. To my subdued 'what a night, sir', he paused only to reply 'oh yes – but we'll soon get over that' before passing on. Night had gone and he had come through once more.

Chapter 8

The Wrath of Battle

As the winter of 1943 set in the soldiers of 78th Division struggled against the German defences on the eastern seaboard of Italy. Eventually the Division was withdrawn to rest after heavy losses. Colin Gunner found his admiration of the Faughs increasing as he watched them return from the line, the 'proud green plumes of Ireland waving' in their head-dress.

THIS ONE was just 'Pop'. Every farm, large or small, smashed or whole, usually had some trembling owner or tenant left behind like a little oyster catcher picking up the pieces when the tide had rolled over his few and often barren acres. He was always old, always unshaven, and always totally dominated by that shapeless black bundle 'Mama'. How we grew to respect those indomitable Mamas at whose age we could only guess.

Hoe in hand, snot-nosed brats underfoot, poking a few thorns under a black pot with only a garish picture of Our Lady on the cracked wall to give them a sense of comfort; we all saluted you Mama, and felt deep down that if we had had to fight Italy's women, we should be swimming back to the safety of Africa.

But Antonio, Garibaldi, Guiseppe, or given a belly or a jaw, Mussolini, received their jocular nicknames before the carrier engines had cooled or the first chicken exploded in a cloud of feathers. This was just 'Pop'; one-eyed, dirty and old, quite alone in a damaged little farm behind the ridge screening us from the mighty Sangro and the waiting defenders of the Winter Line. We had two little buildings and Pop was lucky in that only Jack Tuff, the carrier driver, Jimmy Thorpe, the despatch-rider, Abrahams, the wireless-operator, and my new batman, Boswell, plus myself now came to re-organise his life. The Irish Brigade was in reserve while bridgeheads were being put over the river in rain that never stopped. While Argylls, Kents and Buffs passed days and nights of liquid misery hanging on to a shallow hold and praying for relief, we lived it up in our little forgotten backwater.

We lived pretty well too, on duff, biscuit burgoo and tinned bacon. The company commander was absent for a spell and we received a very odd specimen in his place. As he never came near us and was happy to sit in his billet all day by the fire, this did not bother us, but some days later, after a visit to draw rations, Johnny Bowley reported to me that he could get no sense out of him and that he was sitting counting rusty razor-blades on his table,

43

*Italian civilians return to their homes as the Faughs lead the
Allied advance towards Rome (IWM)*

watched warily by his CSM. Very soon he departed, never to be heard of again, leaving no ripple at all on the little world of 7 Platoon. Thorpe and Pop became very pally and had long chats, Thorpe in Yorkshire dialect and Pop in some form of Italian dating from the Medicis.

Pop soon got the hang of Thorpe who was voted cook. Tuff and Abrahams might be good for the odd Woodbine, Boswell gave him a shirt (one of mine), myself he totally ignored, but Jimmy Thorpe was the man who opened tins, sloshed petrol on the fire, cut loaves and fishes and brewed tea in a black can over Pop's crackling fenceposts and barn doors. Thorpe was 'Mungiari' – per se, Thorpe was God. When planes droned overhead, and he was ordered by Thorpe to get in the cellar as they (pointing skywards) were Tedeschi he did so and never heard the crack of Thorpe's Luger killing another of his dwindling flock of chickens. If he did he enjoyed his share of stewed chicken in his chimney corner that night.

Stirring sounds were heard from Monty now – 'hitting for six', 'giving them a mighty crack', 'The Lord mighty in battles', and so on, and, sure enough, it was considered that the wicket had dried out now and the First Eleven could put on their pads in their warm dry pavilion. What the opening batsmen over the river must have said, and later did say, touched the peaks of blasphemy.

Another little haven had to be left and over the bar the waters looked black and cold. On our last day, I purchased a sheep and a goose – shades of Goose Farm where payment was deferred. The sheep I gave to Johnny Bowley to do mine host to the guncrews of the Platoon, the goose I handed over to Jimmy Thorpe with orders for a farewell feast for our little band and Pop. Vino was obtained by the jerrican and I had a bottle of Jamieson's Whiskey. Thorpe gave his heart to the job and although we all helped he really made old Escoffier rotate in his grave. Pop watched all from his corner out of one runny eye and as any movement on his part only earned him a 'get out of the fucking way, Pop' he soon decided that it was some holy day, sacred to the lunatic Inglesi, and sat and hoped.

We started at six in the evening and as I entered the kitchen I saw the Gran Sasso far away in the mountains with the snows blazing in the sunset while our little valley steamed sodden and slatey. That kitchen was no dream of *bon viveur*, no stars or crossed forks would have been awarded to it; but no chef in tall hat called to the big tables in Claridges could have outshone a Yorkshire pit lad who hacked that goose into six portions and dragged Pop out of his chimney corner to sit on an ammo box with the rest of us. Goose, Maconochie's, M and V bread, apple sauce, then duff covered in treacle was our menu. The best tribute was when it was ended and the little that was shied at the usual mangy cat sent that beast out to look for a mouse as pudding. As I felt this to be the pre-battle banquet and the vino was starting to tell I saw it as my duty to thank and praise Jimmy. This was seconded by a grunt from Jack Tuff and the comment 'Yes, but he makes lousy tea'. Old Pop was made of sterner metal and no sound except his few remaining rotten teeth hard at work came from him. He now understood that we were departing and foresaw less generous guests from some mobile bath unit arriving. But even he had enough in the end and after several tots of cognac he staggered, belching, to bed.

We settled down to the cognac and whiskey and the warmth of the last of Pop's farm cart and it was very late when we sprawled on our blankets by the dying fire. Before the now very drunken Thorpe reeled to his corner, he opened the little hatchway behind which Pop slept on a heap of rags and torn quilts. Crashing his fist down on the heap with a blow that would have settled Marciano, he bellowed 'Goodnight Pop, you poor old bastard'. In my happy haze I muttered 'Mind you don't kill him', but not really caring, fell asleep. As we left at dawn, groping my way to the carrier, I fell in the cesspit; so perhaps the still sleeping Pop had the last word!

A few more days of waiting in the rain, a last glimpse of the two-badged beret in a passing Mercedes car, a night of jitters, being shelled by a high velocity gun, and then we crossed the river. The bridge was wobbly and leaning due to the river rush and shelling, but in uncanny silence we reached the bank and together with the Faughs' carriers made an undignified bolt for the shelter of the escarpment. This was a vertical bank behind which literally everyone hid from the eyes on the ridge some mile ahead, eyes that spoke to batteries of 88s and 105s and sent bangs and black smoke down on what they saw. To my horror I saw that the carriers had halted on the track and were not getting into cover, so I rushed to the front to find out what the hell was going on. There in the moonlight I met the bespectacled and mild Ronnie Wilkin of the Faughs who assured me that, 'cautious soul that I am', he was sweeping the field for mines before crossing.

Day brought activity, orders and noise. I was to go with the Rifles this time and went to find their captain, Rodney Cockburn. As we looked at our route up to Mozzagrogna, crashes on the top of the escarpment and much ducking proved to be the wiping out of an Orders Group and the death of Brigadier 'Swifty' Howlett.

Then the fighter-bombers, five Focke Wulfs, arrived, engines howling. This was unfair, as a vertical bank spelt security; even mortars had a job to hit you behind one, but these bastards came up our kilt from behind. They threw a very effective spanner in the timetable of the 'mighty swipe'. Flint and Corporal Brett, of 6 Platoon, were killed and several others wounded but I got my boys out with the Rifles' carriers and we started off as the barrage opened out and the Skins went over the top, leading the way for the Irish Brigade assault.

We had cleared the escarpment when more Focke Wulfs arrived and we saw thankfully that we had got out just in time. As they hammered the same area a flight of American Kittyhawks jumped them, but those were the heirs to Richthofen and Voss in those German cockpits for they wheeled into the attack and shot their way clear. The air battle was fought almost at ground level and I watched a crippled Kittyhawk with the prop windmilling and the pilot trying desperately to get enough altitude to bale out. His engine suddenly spewed glycol, the plane stalled and the pilot came down with it, his 'chute wrapped around the tail. All he had needed was two hundred feet, but it was not to be. Halted on the road we had dived for the ditch from where, looking up, I saw a Focke Wulf thunder over the column at fifty feet. His canopy was open and he waved to us as he hared for home, his ammunition expended.

We eventually came to a dead stop half a mile from Mozzagrogna. To pass through the village and link up with the Rifles depended on the Gurkhas getting the place; we had been told that they already held it. They had got it, but had then been bounced very smartly out of it by some very tough German paras, assisted by a flamethrower tank. As I joined Rodney Cockburn by his carrier, the Gurkhas seemed to be starting to have another go at the place.

We were joined from nowhere by a Sapper officer of the Indian Division who was off his head with shock and who gave us the creeps, with tales of disaster for this unblooded division. Rodney remained serene, but measured the jump to the ditch with his eye. I could have told him to an inch and also who would be there first. This was the first time I had seen the little men from Nepal in battle and it was a unique view. One lot was being reformed after a good hiding and another battalion was passing through for another attack.

Two figures stayed with me forever. One was on a stretcher hung from a mule; he was far gone and as the mule stopped by me I saw his blood dripping through the canvas and puddling into the ruts. He looked, in that deceptive Gurkha way, about fifteen, and the tears were streaming down his little round face. It was horrible to watch as I could only think of a little boy chastised and lost, running for the arms of his mother. The mule jolted on and when the stretcher was lowered to the ground I felt that his Gurkha mother would have dried his tears forever. The other figure was a Gurkha subadhar leading his men forward, stick in hand, kukri in belt. Up the slope he went, soldierly and stout, every inch of his stocky figure unawed, to vanish in the 'wrath of battle'.

Stop, start, stop, start, until with boiling engines we got into the village square, while the now victorious Gurkhas tried to clear the end of the street. The flamethrower tank was at the corner, burning and exploding, its turret blown off and lying twenty yards away. I was told by survivors that the German officer had sat on the turret directing the counter-attack until some captain of the Royal Fusiliers had fired a PIAT bomb from the window above; exploding in the open hatch it had blown up the tank's ammunition and flame liquid in one tremendous roar. The Fusiliers' captain was a very brave man, but he was killed seconds after this feat.

We got into the house by the tank and pulled the carriers close to the wall. Here we would stay until the street was clear, but Rodney was rightly anxious to get on to join the Rifles and wondered what they were thinking of our delay. I bolted into the house with the platoon and, in the passage, found a little lost Gurkha rifleman who seemed very pleased to see us. Like every British soldier, I had to have a look at his kukri, but he seemed to think that I wanted it and put it back firmly in his sheath.

My handsome Irishman, Sergeant Taylor, active as a farmyard terrier ratting at the rick, spotted this and also assumed that I wanted a kukri. He dived out the back and, despite the sniping, came back with six. He presented me with one and, as I seemed taken aback, showed me, from the backdoor, the garden hedge behind the house. A section of Gurkhas lay alongside it, dead – caught with an enfilade burst of Spandau. They were all minus their kukris. Before I could remark on looting from the dead, Taylor discovered a safe bricked into the wall of a room and was calling for a pick-axe to smash his way to riches. Despite three pick-axes and a burst of Tommy-gun fire, it defied his efforts. The firm of Chubb build a stout product and I wish I had kept the nameplate he wrenched off in a temper.

Outside in the street four Germans lay slain over a limber and by them a German paratrooper lay dead on his back with a woman's photograph held in his lifeless hand before his face. Until that moment I had thought that such things only happened in the films. Meanwhile Sergeant Taylor had found a box of eggs and was sharing them out as I made my way up the street to see what was going on.

I jumped behind a carrier as a bullet hit the tracks and considered life for a minute. Whilst I crouched I glanced to the left and saw in a doorway a German para corporal, complete with Schmeisser, studying me at a range of ten yards. Now, like most, I heeded the advice not to carry anything visible to show I was an officer, such as pistols or mapcases. Thus my Colt automatic, acquired from the sobbing Italian youth, was buttoned inside my battledress blouse and my map was folded in my hip pocket. All very splendid but just try getting a hefty automatic out of an inside pocket in a hurry with two buttons in the way. It works for Chicago gunmen, I know, but not for me. As I did my delving and tugging act the German had enough time to eat a light lunch and still shoot me. Instead, he merely stared at me until I advanced on him brandishing my now accessible six-gun. He then carefully propped his Schmeisser in the doorway and came out, followed by three more. All were lugging artillery with enough firepower to stop a division. As they put up their hands I felt considerable relief.

Waving them ahead and dodging down the street I made a good entrance to the Square, hoping that a general, at least, would be there to see it. 'Ah, my boy, . . . this is MC work . . . proud of you . . .'. Alas, no welcome apart from grinning Gurkhas in doorways and windows until my bomb-happy sapper popped up again. He seemed worse than ever, incoherent and rolling of eye, but not so bad that he did not spot that each German had a good wrist-watch; before my indignant eyes he pinched the lot as I handed the Germans over to a Gurkha Command Post. I never held with looting personal property, except photographs, and remarked 'Fuck you, I caught them' as I left him crooning over his treasures. On my way back up Snipers' Alley I suddenly remembered that German paratroops always had automatic pistols and dashed recklessly for their late hideout. I collided inside with Sergeant Taylor who was grinning happily and holding three brand new Lugers: total gain, one torn blouse with two buttons missing.

Dusk was falling with the last barrage that put the Faughs over the last opposition when we caught up with the Rifles' assault companies. Colin Gibbs, one of their commanders, gave me a mug of tea and after a few caustic comments on the day's battle, sped me to Fossacesia with orders to find John Lofting, the other leading company commander. Fossacesia was eerie in the moonlight, silent and utterly smashed. No wall seemed more than three feet high and there were heaps of ruins everywhere.

Putting two of the guns up on a rubble heap held by a cheerful Rifles sergeant, and hoping I had done right, I found John Lofting below a smashed house in a dugout that was was straight out of 'Journey's End', even to a candle in a bottleneck.

Expecting a blast for being so late I touched my cap to him with some misgivings. He was a well-known 'tough egg' and would have no time for any alibis about being held up or delayed by others' failures. With some relief I was welcomed warmly and offered a drink. This was produced by his runner from a violin case full of captured bottles of Schnapps, carrying which he had faithfully followed his major all through the attack. They had found the case, empty, and the Schnapps in a German dugout earlier in the day and the prudent John had told his runner to fill it and follow him. Any German defender of Fossacesia must have assumed, before he was killed or captured, that the London Philharmonic had been conscripted *en masse*. The drinks were splashed into tin mugs and we were joined in the candlelight by Father Dan, the Brigade's Catholic priest who was very catholic when it came to the hard stuff. John seemed pleased to find a job for Father Dan, as in the corner of that dugout was the only civilian soul I saw on that smashed ridge – an old man on a bunk who was in extremis and at the very gates of Eternity. How he had got there, or why the Germans had let him stay, was a mystery, but there he was and leaving Dan giving him the Last Rites, we went out into what remained of the night.

Peter Grenell and his Company collected me at dawn and we marched forward to a place marked on the map as Rocca. En route the startled German crew of a motorcycle combination leapt off their machine amid a volley of shots from the Rifles and bolted away in the olive groves. I saw that it was one of those magnificent Zundapp machines and hastily detached Corporal Potts to sit on it and defend it from looters or people with a warped sense of property. As Peter Grenell did not claim it, it was mine by divine right of being on it first.

I had envisaged Rocca as another rubble heap on the Fossacesia, Mozzagrogna model, but was amazed to climb up the gully into an untouched little village – not even a welcoming cackle from a foredoomed chicken broke the silence of that sunny October morning as we searched the empty little piazza. The silence was broken by a musical bedlam. Peter's riflemen had found a shop full of saxophones, drums, trombones and other instruments and a hilarious little group, which soon comprised most of the Company, was belting out 'In the Mood'. As only about two of them could play a note, the row was hideous but we all enjoyed it and apart from pianos and sets of drums, which were pretty static, the goods were soon distributed among the 'music lovers'. Jack Tuff, who had once been a bugler, secured a magnificent trumpet. Peter, recollecting that he was conducting a company advance, put a stop to 'In the Mood' and radioed back that Rocca was in our hands. I was far too busy even to pay attention to Johnny Bowley asking for permission to go off and 'investigate' a German dump, as Corporal Potts had roared into the square with *my* Zundapp combination in working order. I had already become the owner of a Fiat saloon car and an Italian motorbike, but gave these away to the doctor when I saw him later. My main obsession was the Zundapp as it gave out its treacly roar, and I schemed to keep this Rolls Royce of vehicles from grabbing seniors. That we had to go on that night was obvious, but the thought of exposing this beauty to danger was out of the question, so I told

Potts to make his way back to B Echelon, tell the Transport Officer it was mine, chain it to his wrist when he slept, and, short of violence, not to give it up even to a full general.

Still 'In the Mood' we pushed on forward, but as the darkness came rain came too and the laden riflemen now found their loot to be a burden. Some was handed to my boys on the carriers with bloodchilling threats in the event of its non-return to the owners, but most was heaved into the ditch. I watched one saxophone, worth many lira in Naples, thrown away with a curse by a soaking and tired rifleman already laden with a Bren gun and pack. Joe Loss would have wept. Very little sleep came that night, only steady sheets of rain and thunder, but a lot of people seemed to have caught us up as we over-looked a large steep wadi at dawn. Tanks of the 17th/21st Lancers were a comforting sight and the always welcome badge of the artillery meant things were back to normal again. When Major Colin Gibbs took his extended Company over the wadi things indeed flicked back to normal as the German 90th Light, of Africa fame, informed their snipers and Spandau crews that enough was enough.

Colin's voice could be heard over the wadi as he tried to get on against much fire from his left, fire which robbed him of his great little Colour-Sergeant Donaghy, MM, killed by a sniper. We opened up from a farm to discourage Colin's opposition and while lying beside Corporal Henshall on No 4 gun I realised we were not the only confused citizens on this wadi. A German Spandau crew of three calmly came round the corner of a barn opposite and assembled their apparatus with their eyes riveted on Colin's Company. Although Corporal Henshall was a very competent No 1, I hastily pushed him to one side and with open sights fired a full belt into these entrepreneurs of battle. My takeover bid was successful and even their Spandau was found in three pieces later on. Their bodies were pepper-pots.

Then a German tank ambled up in full view and six Lancer tanks all fired at it simultaneously. He simply disintegrated in a black cloud as did two lorry-loads of German infantry. This woke the enemy up to our presence and took their eyes off Colin's Company for a moment as they let us have a bit back. Still pounding away with Henshall's now boiling gun, I suddenly heard amid the general noise, a sound like a wet towel hitting the bath and, looking around, saw a melon on a low wall about a foot from my head with a very black hole smack in the centre. That sniper had a choice of two melons when he squeezed his trigger and had chosen the fruit variety. To keep my melon from harm we dragged the gun behind the building and looked for a new site.

While doing this I looked into the farm and found three of the ammo numbers had not wasted a moment to snatch a little bliss. An ancient gramophone, cranked by one, was blaring away with a tune that haunts me now, 'The Lights of Paris'; an Italian woman was giving birth on a bed in a mess of groans, blood and jelly, assisted by another who had harboured medical ambitions in his youth, whilst the third's arse was going like a piston-rod as he copulated on a mattress with a hag old enough to be his granny. They had all found the vino and guzzled it by the jugful. While battle raged a few feet away and the crack of the tank guns made the building shake, they had created a little private oasis of wine, women and song. Adaptability was ever the British soldier's greatest virtue, but this was too much, as I pointed out in lurid language, only to be met with fuddled grins and the use of my Christian name, although Errol Flynn on the mattress did have the decency to disengage. My references to The Army Act were cut short when the mortar crew outside the back window fired and forgot they were under an apple tree; the bomb, happily only a smokebomb for ranging, came smartly back and filled the boudoir/delivery ward with white fog.

Even the 'Lights of Paris' were blotted out. The battle had only been another delaying action, although hectic enough for our taste, to let the Germans get clear of San Vito and back on to the Moro River. I met up in San Vito with the gleaming monocle and Middle Temple accents of Da Pinna, who had been plodding up behind with the Skins. On the Sangro Ridge after a long day he had wearily and in darkness, lain down beside his carrier in a sunken lane and slumbered heavily. At dawn the monocle was ritually jammed in his eye so that turning his head on his pack he had a close view of a dead hand sticking out of the earth inches from his nose. His sleep had been on earth, concealing one whose sleep caused the monocle to drop from his eye – no mean feat. A little later DP had cause to sprint very fast for a handy shell-hole which he entered with a flying leap only to land on a rotted corpse which exploded on impact with his sprawling figure. He did not confide in me if he was wearing his monocle at the time.

As I lounged about in San Vito, temporarily masterless, I was told by the Brigadier to take my Platoon and search all high buildings to see if any death or glory Germans were still hanging about with radios connected to their artillery batteries. Off we went and spent a happy morning rooting about in lofts and attics while Sergeant Taylor acquired more trifles which looked in need of a good home. Eventually I got to the church with its tall campanile. Booting open a side door, and accompanied by six of the platoon, I strode in, cap on back of head and Tommy-gun under arm, to see to my dismay what seemed to be the entire population jammed in the place while a priest at the altar competed with the noise of the guns outside. Scarlet with embarrassment, I pulled off my cap, while Woodbines were pinched out behind me, to be greeted quietly by another priest who opened a side door and showed the entry to the campanile. Oh, Father Dan, where were you?

The Faughs were in battle again soon, getting a bridgehead on the Moro, but after going up to try and find them and being catapulted out of the jeep, as the driver dodged a near miss, I was told that, at long last, the Irish Brigade was being pulled out and the entire Division was being relieved by the Canadian 1st Infantry. The 78th Division had sustained 10,000 casualties in six months which, in plain language, meant that the climbers of Calvary, the infantry battalions, were no longer effective and even we humble footmen to the great had gaps in our ranks. It was time to go home for Christmas, to count heads and rejoice. With Jack Tuff driving the carrier and blaring his looted trumpet at every stop and halt, we turned away. We rattled back through San Vito passing alongside the trudging files of tired Rifles, Faughs and Skins; files which were smaller than usual and often led by strange faces. I felt very proud to be greeted by some with a friendly wave as they plodded on, the green plumes of Ireland flying in their caubeens and a company piper playing 'Paddy Dear' ahead of them. If I had passed C Company of the Faughs I would have felt otherwise perhaps. At the last moment, as they held on to their bridgehead and fought off a counter-attack, Death had found Tommy Wood. 'Get up, you yellow bastard' still rang in my ears.

Mortar carriers of the Faughs on the road to Rome pass a five-barrelled
mortar abandoned by the Germans (IWM)

Chapter 9

Military Hospital

78th Division's rest kept most of the formation out of the line over Christmas 1943 but while they were resting Colin Gunner found himself in hospital, first with pneumonia and then with jaundice.

THE OLD Sangro battlefield, which we reached at dusk, was transformed now. Dumps and parks of vehicles had given it a look of permanence and peace. Where the Skins had crouched under Li Colle and Major Bobby Greer had given the order to his CSM: 'Tell them to put those bits of tin on the end of their rifles', Canadian echelon troops now wandered around and searched for souvenirs in the trenches and bunkers. Some hope, after the Irish Brigade had passed that way, I thought, but good luck to them. When we were directed by a military policeman we all knew that we were really out of that other world that lay 'forward of the gun line'. Resigned to a night in the open, we found a beaten-up farm that gave us some shelter and laagered for the night. A fire, brew-up and some grub completed the universal happiness; a happiness made perfect for me when out of the mist and rain an immaculate and testy Brian Clark loomed up with the angry demand: 'Where in hell am I?' From the look on his jeep driver's face as he departed, I knew that two of us would cherish the memory of that military paragon, the Adjutant of the Faughs, getting lost on his way out of the line.

A friendly captain of the Canadian Service Corps wandered in and kindly asked if we needed anything. We gave him a mug of tea and a seat on a hastily-covered case of 'Sockeye Salmon' packed 'with a wiggle in its tail', according to the label. Two of those cases had been lifted from the Canadian dump only ten minutes before by my chaps. I had no sensibilities now as regards such matters and accepted a carton of Sweet Corporals without a qualm. Nobody was going to shoot the Canadian captain's melon full of holes was my thought.

Before we departed next day, despite Corporal Potts' loud objections, I tried my hand on the Zundapp combination. Used only to army motorbikes, I revved up, went into a tight circle and hit a tree. With a bruised knee and ignoring Potts' blasphemous version of 'I told you so', I led the little column off southwards, passing our decent Canadian officer, who must have noticed that every man was breakfasting on Sockeye Salmon, tins jagged open and contents eaten with jack-knives.

As the carriers ran well and the road was well marked, boredom soon set in, which I enlivened by taking potshots at the circling shitehawks in a clear autumn sky. I soon stopped this entertainment when Johnny Bowley in the rear entered into the spirit of things by spraying the blue with a captured Spandau mounted on his carrier. During a halt the Platoon bad character nodded towards a single grave at the roadside and remarked to me: 'Bit lonely for him, ain't it? Can't even roll over and have a chat with his mate'. As dark came I transferred to my cherished Zundapp sidecar and wrapped in a blanket, with fur collar pulled over my face, prepared for a warm cosy journey.

Sleep, assisted by frequent swigs of the 'water' bottle soon came and despite the biting cold and roar of the machine, I quitted the troublous world for ten minutes. Only a dream I thought, as my foggy mind registered flames in my face and smoke in my lungs, but not a dream as Potts stopped hastily and hit me smartly across the face with his heavy gloves. After much heaving, cursing and arm flapping, I emerged like a cork from a bottle with pieces of charred blanket and singed fur around my neck. The end of Potts' cigarette had blown off in the night wind and, settling on the blanket, had ignited me as I dreamed with my martial cloak around me. I thought unworthily, that this was Potts' revenge for my morning attempt to ride his/my treasure, but his obvious concern over the scorched paintwork assured me. We realised that we were alone on the road and it was a very cold still night. With a creep of fright, I also realised that we were by the Trigno bridge,and in the middle of that wood of horrors. Two pulls at the bottle, a kick of the starter and we fled over the now new Bailey Bridge. Too many ghosts beckoned from those twisted, icy trees for my comfort.

All next day we rumbled on, now climbing into the hills and we were glad to clamber off the carriers at last in the village of San Marco in the Gargano peninsula. Here we re-organised and re-fitted; here we lived on fried chicken and chips with much vino to wash it down; here we were snowed in with a fall of five feet in one storm and supplied, as if that were needed, by an airdrop which, of course, fell two miles away. And here Private Starker had his first grind with *Leather Tits*, the whore who ministered to the entire company. Her collection of soap and ration chocolates was enough to stock *Woolies* according to Sergeant Bowley.

When roads became usable again I visited San Giovanni to see David Davison, an officer in another company. David had been at the same OCTU as myself at York, but was a Green Jacket, so of course we had never met. Now, as officers in the same battalion, those distinctions, so important back on the drill square, had vanished and I loved the company of this quiet, cultured and very intelligent friend who forgave me my snide references in the past to 'those black buttoned bastards from Eton'.

David gave me tea in their Mess and talked of the village priest who was alleged to bear the stigmata. My only contact with miracles so far had been the bursting of a 105 behind instead of on top of me, so with no thoughts at all of marks of Divine Grace, but only in a spirit of vulgar nosiness, I went to see a little figure in his church who wore mittens as he offered the Mass. That evening, with all the clear wisdom of a twenty-one year old, non-church going, nominal Protestant, I explained the whole thing to my own satisfaction, and to Norman Wimbury, a newly arrived officer of the Manchesters. As Norman was much keener to see *Leather Tits* he did not make the pilgrimage to San Giovanni to see that little priest, later so famous and revered, Padre Pio.

Here too, a story passed around the company which rocked discipline to its foundations. Two fusiliers of the Irish Brigade had gone absent or, as was then the offence, 'deserted in the face of the enemy'. After the Sangro battle, brought back to their battalion with a heavy escort of Red Caps, they were dragged before their Colonel under the icy stares of Adjutant and RSM. Both old soldiers, both Irish of the bogs, they stood hatless and battered about the face as a massive list of charges was read out. 'Being in a brothel area, resisting arrest, drunk, striking a superior officer, desertion, plunder'; all were reeled off in an endless litany that amazed even the RSM, hardened by the years to all known crimes.

One spoke for both when asked how he pleaded and answered in a firm and unabashed voice: 'Guilty'. He spoke for both too, when asked if he had anything to say before the inevitable remand for Court Martial and disgrace. He *had* something to say, and all the glory of Ireland's lost causes and defeats rang in his voice as he staked his all on the last throw of the dice. 'You mind that night on the Trigno, Sir, the night we lost the Colonel and the old Battalion? Well, Sir, as I lay in me little slit trench and the stuff was coming down all over us I said to me friend here, "Mac, if I ever gets out of this, I'm going on the piss". And, Sir, *I've been!*'.

The Wild Geese must have sounded the bugles as the Colonel, head in hands on his table, fought to control his laughter and tears. Eventually he won and ordered 'Get out of here, go back to your Company'. And under the thunderstruck gaze of the Red Caps, those magnificent gamblers marched out. Later, the spokesman deserted again: wounded and discharged from hospital he ignored orders to report to a Reinforcement Depot and '*deserted*' forward to his battalion on the lethal slopes of Monte Cassino.

As I had feared, my roaring around in my personal Zundapp had drawn attention. Also, it had drawn resentment from those above with whom I was not too generous with respect. Orders came to hand it over to the Intelligence Officer as he had no jeep. Corporal Potts rose again to the occasion as he handed it over with an assortment of scrap iron in the cylinder. The engine blew up as the new owner started it: petty and spiteful perhaps, but such little trophies did mark the distinction between those who wandered in the twilight zone and those who wore out chinagraph pencils.

Christmas Day came with an awful meal in a filthy village, but as someone had discovered how to make a dangerous punch with vino and wood alcohol, this did not matter. While carol singing with an hilarious Dicky Gray of the Mortars, I even found myself being sociable to Brian Harpur, a major I disliked. 'For malt does more than Milton can, to justify GOD'S ways to man'. My last memory was collapsing on my bedroll in an onion store reciting 'This precious stone set in a silver sea; this earth, this realm . . .'. I awoke with pneumonia.

Military hospitals never had at that stage the fascination that they had the next winter, when they seemed objects of desire so I was not too pleased when, cured of my pneumonia in the Casualty Clearing Station in Campobasso, the Irish sister took one look at a bottle I had filled to order and remarked happily: 'You've got *it* as well. General Hospital for you'. *It* was jaundice, a plague which swept the division. In the ambulance going back to Bari I kept thinking that someone would muck about with No 7 Platoon in my absence. Once in bed in a warm and well filled ward I enjoyed it, after feeling ill for twenty-four hours. Treatment seemed to be to stay in bed and consume vast quantities of sugar. Life was brightened up by two Guards' officers in nearby beds both with gunshot wounds. They conducted private conversations in loud confident tones, when not reading old copies of the *Daily Mirror*. One asked of his chum one morning: 'What became of your brother?' 'Oh, he let the family down badly, he's a major in the Gunners'. A paper rustled opposite and an artillery colonel glared over it at the two types, who of course were not even aware of his existence.

Daily, a large guardsman reported to them and received details of their wants and needs. Daily, the ward shook as he crashed to attention, bellowed 'Sir' and departed. Most of the wants were for local goodies, and choice Chianti. The hospital food was poked listlessly with a fork and largely ignored. The sister they treated with friendly jollity. Daily, we were inspected by the Boss Doctor complete with red tabs and full colonel badges. Daily, I hoped to hear 'Lie to attention', but it never came. When he entered one morning the first object bang in his line of sight was a blue-pyjama-ed backside sticking over the open window ledge. With the aid of some string,

Guardee was hauling up a basket of tuck brought by his batman in the street below. The basket safe in his arms he acknowledged the crash and bellow of 'Sir', then turned and greeted the red-tabbed glare with 'Ah, good morning, Colonel. Just doing a little shopping'. I was sorry to leave that ward, but not sorry to be hitch-hiking back to the platoon next day with the final orders from the Doctor fresh in my mind – 'No alcohol for six months'. As Johnny Bowley would say: 'I should coco'.

After the battle. 2nd London Irish Rifles at Casa Sinagoga, May 1944 (Author)

Chapter 10

The Road to Rionero

Early 1944 and the 78th Division return to the snow-covered mountains. During their time there Colin Gunner was assessed by the Faughs following his request to transfer to them. After a relatively quiet time the Division is moved out. This time it is moving westward and its destination is CASSINO.

IT WOULD have upset that well-meaning doctor if he could have joined, as I did, a party of Buffs' officers that night in the 'Royal York' in Campobasso. Gin was the only drink available; good stuff, too, if you ignored a blue petroleum film on the top, and called *Silver Fizz*.It silvered that tatty little tavern for the Buffs and me and even cast a golden glow on the future as a Buffs lieutenant fell amidst the drums whilst conducting the inevitable, always demanded and never wearied of, *'Lili Marlene'*. If, in 1917, to the pilgrim coming out of the line, Heaven consisted of Amiens, a bath, whiskey, and the *'Long, Long Trail a Winding'*, we could match it with Campobasso, a bath, *Silver Fizz* and *'Lili Marlene'*. Neither of us would have felt out of place if a time machine had clicked forward or back.

As for that tune, bawled, bellowed, hummed and adapted to a hundred different units' words, it was the only piece of loot belonging to the old Eighth Army which has endured. Lugers have been swopped and sold; watches have stopped; cameras taken to the second-hand mart; badges now emblazon teenage belts but the intangible remains. Forget it, Vera Lynn, and you disc makers; it had to be sung in a Naples dive by a sixteen stone Italian, busting her black satin all over the cleavage or noisy and off-key by a muddy platoon in a rest billet, although Father Dan did tell me that it had moved him deeply to hear it the night of the Mareth attack, being taken up all along the German positions just before the barrage came down.

Whenever there's a battle to break the German line,
There you will be certain to see the Shamrock sign,
Oh Mister Churchill, when do we go home,
Now that we have opened the bloody road to Rome?

Monty may have kept his treasures locked in his caravan; his army had *Lili Marlene* locked in their hearts.

61

Isernia, I was told, was the next stop, further still up the great peaks of the Abruzzi, and the gleam of D P's monocle welcomed me back to the Company and invited me to share his billet. After reporting to a new major, Philip Marshall, I was relieved to be told that No 7 Platoon was once more my property after a spell under a strange individual christened by the Platoon 'Alderman Joseph O'Toole', who departed to the Skins. Philip told me that, next day, I was to take 7 Platoon up to Rionero to join the Faughs in the line. Johnny Bowley, the real commander, seemed pleased to see me back and, apart from a few new faces, the old crowd seemed intact, so I spent the night with D P in a very well-organised billet; a night that became famous as the occasion of *'Fudger's Revolt'*.

Fudger was the Company clerk (what's in a name?). Fudger was small and bespectacled; Fudger was polite and neat; Fudger knew his place; above all, Fudger dreaded the word that would wrench him away from his files and rolls, from his endless cups of tea and the roof that did not leak; the word that would send executive Fudger, the *confidant* of sergeant-majors, back to an icy carrier in the rain or a muddy gunpit on a hill. But Fudger fell among thieves that night; thieves of the vino-punch drinking breed, who plied Fudger with mugs of the stuff until, with hair rumpled, jacket ripped open and spectacles misted, he threw open the door of the officers' billet and surveyed D P, Teddy Cullen, Norman Wimbury and myself, with a long look of lofty contempt. He then, with an orderly precision and starting with the senior officer, Teddy Cullen, delivered a thumbnail sketch of each officer's character, courage, ability and personal habits with a rich background of anecdote and detail gleaned over the months. Nothing was missed, nothing was spared us and nothing would have stopped Fudger as he declaimed his long pent-up diatribe. As he reached his peroration, the CSM came in with some papers for Teddy's signature and, to our delight and relief, Fudger shifted his aim and it was the CSM's turn to know himself. Before he could reveal the real story behind the CSM's visit to hospital in Algiers, and much to our disappointment, his collar was seized by the CSM and he got the bum's rush amid cheers and laughter. It was three days before he came into public view again, but a long time before he was allowed to forget the night of his revolt when he had made a little holiday in his heart.

The road to Rionero snaked and twisted and always rose higher into the sea of peaks, but the sun shone and some of the marching troops had their jackets slung that warm and spring-like morning until the sky filled like a cistern, the day became twilight, and the wind, the child of Heaven, came bellowing and crying down from the now invisible heights. Snow we had never dreamed existed hit us, flakes that hissed on the engine covers, hissed, hit again, and choked exhausts and vents; snow that blotted out the carrier in front and drove the marching troops into the lee of any vehicle that could be seen in the white, grey, black bedlam of whistles and wind squalls.

Every carrier became its own little world, every man his own igloo as we struggled on to Rionero and hoped for cover and warmth. The Germans had denied us that by the simple means of attaching a Teller mine to every wall in the village and exploding them. To rub it in they had written up: 'Hope you like your winter billets, Tommy', on the signpost outside the village. So it was, that when we did slither into the village it only resembled a white ruin with the odd wall or chimney sticking up out of the drifts. Those who got there scratched around like weasels for some hole to burrow in or simply slung a cover over the carriers and, running the engines until the petrol gave out, crouched in them all night.

I ploughed my way to a larger than usual ruin and found a small shelter between a broken wall and a square mound of snow. There, Boswell and I made a bedouin lean-to of gascapes and groundsheets and shivered our way into some sort of arctic coma. We awoke in a great white cathedral of soaring mountains. Ironically enough we had pitched our shelter in the smashed church and had crouched behind the altar all night. In icy sunshine, under a metallic blue sky, the nightmare of the darkness faded and we found that, despite their thoroughness, the Germans had not destroyed every scrap of cover.Boxes could be used to plug holes, carriers could be moved alongside smashed walls, sheets could be anchored down to make a roof, even snow could be shovelled up in windbreaks and I think we really enjoyed that day of homebuilding in the white silence of the Abruzzi. The last thought in any-one's mind was of the enemy or his whereabouts. Survival and creature warmth override all dangers and I am sure a primitive man risked a dinosaur's displeasure to carry his firepot into a better cave.

Searching for Boswell to send him on some errand I found him with two others engaged in dropping flaming rags down a hole in our blown-up church. Joining the party I saw that they had discovered a manhole to the crypt and in the light of the rags were viewing the skeletons of long dead citizens of Rionero, all a-jumble in the depths. 'Very interesting – now run off and get Sergeant Bowley' was my only comment to those scientific seekers, but not before I too had had a good look at mummified torsos and brown pelvis bones, and told my 'bad character' that he 'could certainly sleep down there if he felt like it' and he would anyway, in God's good time.

Johnny Bowley was discovered by tracing shouts coming from a round hole like a chimney in a snow-filled ditch. Johnny's body, all five foot four of it, had drilled the chimney when he stepped off the road and went straight

On Monte Grande. A mule carrying supplies to the Faughs loses its footing on the ice. January 1945 near San Clemente (IWM)

down into the snow. His description of his feelings as he shot down into the depths would have earned him a seat with Demosthenes.

It was homely when night fell and the great crests glistened in the moon and starlight to hear the old familiar banshee wail of the pipes as Brian Clark ordered the duty piper to play *'Officers' Mess'* outside their shored-up cowshed and let the world know that tempests may rage but the machine of the Regiment grinds on, and it was to this lamplit hovel that a written note bade me report for dinner. I had applied some time before to transfer to the Faughs battalion and this summons was to let them have a look at what sort of a lunatic was actually asking to get a bit further forward and nearer to sudden death.

However, Major Holmes, their second-in-command, made me welcome and gave me bully fritters and spuds while Brian watched in the lamplight to see if I could use a knife and fork. I must have passed muster as I was given a drink and told to report next day to go off and dig positions for an incoming company of the Skins. We had a picnic outing that next day with mugs clanking and packets of bully and bread, building shelters for the Skins and even putting up a couple of tents. We had done a fair job as Major Adrian Cooke remarked when he arrived with his sweating company.

I sent the Platoon off home at once and they disappeared down the slope, shovels clinking and still heaving the odd snowball at Abrahams. I lingered with Adrian and his South African lieutenant, Jackson, and had some of his rum. I lingered too while the sun lit the mountaintops and the valleys filled with grey, but what the hell, there was only one track back to a fire and supper and I knew the way. So, with the first stars now out I set off and heard the domestic sounds of Adrian's company fade behind me as, warmed with his rum, I listened to the total silence and the crunch of my boots on the snow. Then a wolf howled. That awful wail that echoed over the shattering silence stopped me dead with animal fear. Hair and spine fused and my bowels turned to icy slush. No matter that I had a Tommy gun, enough to slay a pack of wolves, that sound that seemed to hang on the echoes filled me with sheer terror. It was like a lost soul crying in Eternity. The trot I broke into became a run as I fled towards Rionero, when I saw, and saw absolutely clearly, a man, rifle at his shoulder, kneeling in the snow, aiming at me. One wild dive off the track and soaking and freezing I awaited a German patrol. Hours seemed to pass until I ventured a look up again at the track; he was still there, but had changed into a cairn of stones with the snow drifted against one side.

I arrived at Rionero at a speed that Roger Bannister never touched later and crashed into the fire's glow with a shirt soaked inside with sweat and outside with snow. Jack Tuff looked at me oddly but said nothing as I spooned down my Maconochies with a hand that still shook. It was all those damned mountains, I thought later; by day in sunshine and by night in the moonlight they loomed above the little black dots busy making war on their skirts. They magnified, rolled around, and toyed with the odd gun salvo that was fired, and then, contemptuously tossing it aside, brooded on. Wherever one looked they were there and it was a change to gaze down the valley to the Sangro river at the bottom. That at least was familiar; we knew all about it but even the Cockneys, armoured with their memories of buses, traffic and Marble Arch in the rush hour, seemed overawed by the setting.

Down to the river nightly went *Creeping Jesus* as some wit had christened him. This was an officer detailed to go to the river and measure its depth with a sort of crucifix rod and pole. What good this did, apart from giving the unhappy man pneumonia, no-one knew, but it brightened up the platoon settling down in the new habitable holes and burrows of the Rionero warren. Wild stories began to come up with the rations, tales of Poles who brought fur-clad women into the line with them and scaled peaks, knives in teeth. All well garnished rubbish as it turned out, but it was a romantic thought to be relieved by the Carpathian Lancers and to see those warrior exiles who had a double-headed white eagle to march beneath. They had precious little else, existing on the cast-offs of charity, except an abundance of courage. And that they had in overwhelming measure. But to us, they were just another funny unit to take over our now happy little village, riddled with fully detached and individual fug-holes.

Farewell to those mountains and snow we thought, as we headed back to Isernia and farewell to heart-stopping wolves, I thought secretly. A glance at a contour map of Italy would have soon disabused us, but that would come later on. In the meantime, the old familiar arrows surmounted with the Golden Chopper of the Divisional sign guided us down. But the snow did not let us escape so easily and in a miniature blizzard we halted in the late afternoon by some railway cottages where Johnny Bowley informed me that the civilians did not wish to let us into their shelter. That was soon solved by three blows of a battering ram formed from a concrete railway sleeper on the back door, and snow-dusted, cold and in no mood for chats with our new allies I told Johnny to brew up in the kitchen and Boswell to get some wood, any wood, and get a fire going in the tiny parlour. Antonio and his brood thought the SS had arrived and even Mama, the indomitable, looked a bit scared as the platoon filled the rooms and covered the kitchen in trodden snow and dixies. A good place for the night, we thought, looking out at the flakes and gloom. Tea and stew confirmed our impression. I had recovered my temper by then and, seated by the parlour fire in an easy chair, got up when a girl came into the room. She was I suppose the daughter of the family and she sat quietly in the other chair, knitting. Probably sent in by Mama to placate the English Himmler, I thought, as the darkness came, the fire crackled and her telegraph pole needles clicked. I fell into an amazing dreamlike state, half asleep, looking at the shadows on the scabby wall and the girl knitting by the fire. This is what it must be like to be married and settled down in life kept running through my brain. This is what we are supposed to be like; this room is what the rules say should always exist for ever and ever. I do not know if it was a dream or thought; I do know that I could no more have touched that girl than cut my own throat with a blunt bayonet. I did not want her but I wanted that picture that the room and she made when occasionally she looked up and smiled timidly at my slouched figure steaming in the chair. Perhaps it was only minutes that lengthened like shadows but I never forgot the room or her and felt almost like crying when Boswell came and said the company commander wanted me.

In the snowy dark he dashed our cosy plans; all to move at once, no stopping that night; no stopping next day come to that. The whole Division was on the move, westwards, and for the first time there came from his lips the word that was to fill our whole world, that was to fill our lives, our fears – and our prayers in the weeks to come; the word which was to be the last geography for so many, as the dark lodestone beckoned ahead. *'We are going to Cassino'*

Chapter 11

'Lachrymae Christi'

The Cassino position, the anchor of the Germans' Gustav Line, had enabled the Germans to stop the Allied advance south of Rome. Attempts to break through had been repelled at great loss and an amphibious landing at Anzio had been made in an effort to break the deadlock. That had failed due to the timidity of the American commander and General Alexander had now moved most of his troops from the east of Italy to the west in preparation for an offensive that would finally break the Gustav Line.

ALL THE events on the other side of Italy, shielded from us by the Apennines, might as well have been taking place in Burma, as with a certain air of patronising expertise we camped around Capua. Fifth Army indeed – some bunch of bunglers who had cocked up Salerno and let the Germans blow up the post office in Naples was our total and devastating summary of their bloody days from the beaches to the Garigliano and now before the slopes of Cassino. Those wearing the Africa Star mentally patted the heads of those well-meaning but fumbling small boys from the lower third, and firmly referred to all gullies as wadis; corduroys, a badge of the desert army, were obligatory in Naples' clubs.

Our company had the run of an olive orchard with not so much as a barn to play with. All those buildings had been collared by the Faughs across the road to keep their bagpipes dry. Sandy soil was our reward as the bivouacs were dug in and some of the platoon reached coalmine depths before calling a halt. Invited into one I went down seemingly endless steps into a little snug room, six feet deep, complete with shelves cut in the walls and candles on brackets, to share a mug of tea with two gun numbers, gentlemen who, in the past, had to be under shellfire before using a shovel. Boswell did me proud with a rainproof effort although I did not rate shelves and light fittings.

The road ran back to Caserta, where the mighty of Allied Forces HQ lived in four-poster beds with halls of mirrors in the palace, and then on to Naples. It was a busy road which through all of one day and night carried the wheeled might of a mechanised America, when the 88th Division, the Blue Devils, rolled past to the line; a perfect convoy, a full-strength division, with not a rifle or a brew-can hanging from a mirror-bracket. It was a long straight road which provided much sport for those gay souls who flew the little artillery

The Adjutant, Brian Clark, sent a piper out to play in the snow.
Christmas 1944 (IWM)

spotter planes. Before landing on their cabbage patch they amused themselves by flying inches above and behind a laden lorry before dropping down to ground level in front of the bulging eyes of the driver. Sometimes they tried this trick head-on, only bouncing over the cab at the last second but this drew a rebuke down on the aerial acrobats and it was stopped.

Training for river crossing in assault boats was ordered on the rapidly flowing Volturno. In battle order we assembled boats, clambered in and listened in bored attitudes to an RE sergeant giving instructions. We knew all about it, thought Ratty, Mole and Badger, while I donned Toad's mantle and sat in the sharp end with a rope and spike to leap ashore and anchor the vessel. Leap I did, but no-one had told me the Volturno had vertical banks and, clutching my spike, I went to the bottom. Johnny Bowley who was coxing the eight told me later what the RE sergeant said as I disappeared in the depths while the boat spun out of control, and if I had not been wet and cold I would have gone back and put him on a charge.

We did an exercise with the Faughs but only got very wet before a bored Jimmy Clarke, one of their majors, called it off. I returned with him to their BHQ in the farm and joined a throng around the fire, steaming and scrounging tea. The best places were occupied by Colonel Jimmy Dunnill, Brian Clark and Pixie Brown, the Signals' Officer, so when an artillery lieutenant at the back had lit his pipe he flicked the match over the heads of the crowd towards the fire. As it passed over the little gathering it made a loud whirr and hiss that to every ear meant only one thing, a shell arriving and a close one at that. Those reflexes, trained and tuned in a hundred like moments, were like razors. Seats crashed over as all dived flat and I was almost proud to think that I was under the table before any. The author of the outrage stood vertical and solitary, puffing placidly on his pipe. In silence and with shifty looks, seats were resumed and figures emerged from under tables. Brian spoke for all of us as he nailed the pipe-puffer with a frozen glare and said with great emphasis: 'Never do that again'.

Parties from each company were allowed into Naples on day trips and with Jack Oliver, an Argentinian, I went to see the Bay, hear Santa Lucia and buy a musical box. Before departing we stocked up on Durex and Dreadnoughts, hoping for the big occasion and very nearly made it in some gin mill where I urged Ollie to use the power of his wallet to convince two crows in black that he was Senor Fray Bentos in person. All went well for a while and we were both eyeing the curtain that led upstairs and ordering Asti Spumanti by the hogshead when two majors of a US Bomber Group came in and with croaks of delight the crows flew off to their table. Majors, and with flight pay – even Ollie's wallet could not compete with that, so with baffled curses we slunk out and sought the Officers' Club. Here we were on safer ground as the singer, always alleged to have been Kesselring's mistress, belted out *Chiri Biri Bim*. Here I met *Lachrymae Christi*.

Joining three others at lunch I passed sneering comments on the size of the bottle and ordered four; then four more. The others I believe went on to see the Via Roma; I awoke at teatime in the barber's shop, having had three haircuts, several shampoos and facial towels and two manicures. My muttered *'Encora'*, still aimed at the wine-waiter, was cheerfully interpreted by the scissors' artist as the green light to run up an astronomical bill. I paid up and mentally bracketed *Lachrymae Christi* with banana liqueur. We returned, not even having glimpsed the Bay, to Capua, in a comatose state and even the red glow in the sky of the great Vesuvius eruption did not awaken any interest.

Units of the Division were going into the line to do longstop for the New Zealand and Indian assault on Cassino, due any day now. D P and his platoon departed to sit on the Rapido river near the town and I was quite pleased to have a day off to take him up some rations. My rear echelon ardour slumped when, getting near the famous Mad Mile, I saw for the first time, the backdrop of the theatre that no feat of memory will ever erase.

The day before, a stream of silver Fortresses had thundered overhead, then flight after flight of medium-bombers had trundled back and forth, and from our little grove we had looked up and agreed that once New Zealand had occupied the crater blown in the German line we should be motoring along the Appian Way and putting a Bailey over the Tiber before leaving Father Dan behind to put the Pope right on his theology. Used only to our Monty shuttle service of medium-bombers, that lot looked almost too much of a good thing.

I found D P down a track, in a fortress-like farm, but apart from thinking that the New Zealand guns were going pretty hard, did not, in my euphoria, feel at all interested in the crucifixion down the road. To be told loudly to 'get that bloody jeep out of the way and get in here quick' by our dignified Scot was a bit of a shock, when his unshaven and agitated face appeared in a cellar opening. When I joined him in his cellar and noticed in several of his platoon the old signs of 'the jumps' I took more interest in the surroundings. D P was clearly on edge. 'They put two hundred shells on this place this morning; half the bloody bombing fell short . . . everything can be seen from the Monastery . . . fatal to move in daylight . . . fixed lines everywhere'. This coming from D P was not to be dismissed with a cheery smile and a packet of mail from my pocket. He soon filled in the details, and motoring to Rome was not one of them. His seat in the front row of the stalls gave him a view very different from my hitherto casual squint through opera glasses.

A few nights earlier as he watched the riverbank from the loft of a small house, he had been galvanised to glance down and see under his eaves a German officer calmly calling the roll of his raiding party. Leaving two men below in the ground floor of D P's observation post, the German then set off and clobbered a nearby company, taking several prisoners, before recrossing the river to his own side. D P and Chitty, his batman, had spent an anxious hour holding their breath upstairs while the Wehrmacht sat below. By now I was betraying all the symptoms of front line visitors: 'should love to stay but . . .'; 'better be getting back . . . wonder where I am'; 'sure you have all you need?' and other well-worn preludes to getting the hell out of it. And it was with the foot a little harder on the accelerator that I left him. Reaching the road I saw an overturned and burning jeep further up the bank. It had not been there when I arrived earlier but before really going into my Monza circuit act I was hailed from the roadside. It was a cavalry officer, who had been a brother cadet at Blackdown OCTU in England. Now a Corps Liaison Officer he was the very man to impart details of the grand design. He would surely know more than the shell-battered ones in D P's cellar. He was looking down from Olympus and spoke with generals.

After a quick precis of our mutual military careers he spoke *ex cathedra*: 'See those red smokeshells near the Monastery?' I did indeed, and also many other shellbursts both there and on Hangman's Hill. 'Well, that's marking the Gurkha positions – for an airdrop. We shall be through tomorrow'.

Two months later the shellbursts were falling in exactly the same place, but I was not to know that then. I shot off to Capua to pass on this nugget of inside information.

*The author at his pig-stye Platoon HQ on Monte Grande during the
winter of 1944/45 (Author)*

Chapter 12

The Eyes of the Abbey

A major offensive against the Cassino positions has failed in spite of the courage of the New Zealand and Indian troops. As spring arrives the soldiers of 78th Division wait for yet another assault on Monte Cassino and its ruined monastery, held by the redoubtable Fallschirmjaeger, the German paratroopers.

WE WERE not through tomorrow, nor the next day. We were stopped. We were beaten. All that storm of steel, all those guns, all that courage had foundered, slowed and ground to a halt in the craters of the town and on the slopes of the Hill and a chill came among us as we realised that this time it was not Fifth Army being thrashed, but the elite of the desert. All believed the quoted German intelligence report 'the enemy are using New Zealanders; they therefore mean business'. All knew that a Gurkha Brigade had not stormed the Monastery and the lofty 'Show them how to do it' spirit that we had brought from Africa now sputtered and died. The Division moved into the line to relieve and once more No 7 was allotted to the Faughs.

Surprise now piled upon surprise. All trucks, carriers and other transport were left. A few jeeps, entrusted to the best drivers, were allowed for each battalion and for the rest, mules and muscle.

It was a racing relief for the valley had to be crossed and the mountain climbed before day came and the hidden eyes on the Hill enforced stillness. This was a wide and lonely valley where no bird sang or mouse stirred by day, but profuse with corn and poppies and alive at night with ingoing troops, ration parties, stretcher jeeps and endless muletrains. At night I crossed with the Faughs officers to spy out the land before the companies followed us the next night. And halfway across, stopped with silent engines and noisy hearts, I saw the nodal point of it all; the ruin that towered above, that drew every eye by day and night; the ruin that never for a second in those weeks was out of our thoughts. It seemed, like Silver's parrot, to be perched on our shoulder: the Abbey of St Benedict. Lit by the flames that never stopped, red, green, white, thumping, thudding and simmering like a great black foundry it stared down at us. I had seen it often by day in the shifting smoke clouds and black geysers of flame with its hundred eye sockets empty and black but the first

Tony Morris, 2nd i/c of the Faughs at St Patrick's Barracks, Forli on St Patrick's Day (celebrated on March 29th) 1945, just before the final advance over the Senio (Author)

glimpse at night was the most malevolent as flare chased flare and Jack Broadbent of the mortars assured me that three reds meant a big bombardment and we were in the open.

Cairo village at the foot of the mountain. a hideous, stinking heap, was cleared safely and, still in jeeps, we climbed the hill on a ghost of a track until a building stopped us and we were there at last. No accents of colonials or muttered Gurkhali greeted us, no homely British dialect spoke in the dark, only a precise French voice that intimated that 'Mon Colonel' awaited us within. We were relieving a *Tabor*, or battalion, of *Goums*, those barbaric warriors of the Atlas, brought across the Narrow Seas to add another page of *La Gloire* to the story of French arms. The colonel and Brian probably got an aperitif and a *Sole Bonne Femme*; Jimmy Clarke, D Company's major and I got orders to go with a muletrain further up to contact '*M'sieur le Capitaine*', who lived in a gully – sorry, wadi.

Jimmy Clarke, a veteran and courageous soldier/barrister (why were all lawyers good soldiers?), knowing his Company contained many rum lovers, had brought the demijohn of happiness with him and, fixing it personally to a mule saddle, he adjured the Algerian bandit in charge to 'prenez garde, c'est tres precieuse' and told me to stick close to the brute of a mule that had already lashed out and missed me by an inch. Only half an hour of winding and climbing took us to Le Capitaine's sangar at the head of the gully. Silence here was absolute, but as Jimmy crawled into the hole I saw that at least they had a candle inside; no other flicker or gleam showed anywhere except the moon on wet rocks, dull equipment and shattered sodden trees. Jimmy had murmured 'watch that jar' as he crawled in, so I stood hand on jar in the dripping dark while the mule piddled and snorted. Here we were conversing in whispers, while this big, four-legged, long-eared sod announced our arrival to any interested German listening post.

I eyed the nearby Goums in their sangars and shelters and as they returned the stare Wellington's comment came to life – 'I don't know what they do to the enemy, but by God they frighten me'. Not without relief I obeyed a whispered 'come inside' from Jimmy and, clutching the rum jar like a chalice, joined him in the sangar, a tight fit, with the two of us, two French officers and 'la precieuse'.

Jimmy, thank God, spoke fluent French and had already got the layout of the gully in his head. Whilst he told me that the gully ended in a sort of rampart where I should put two Vickers, I studied the two French officers in the well-screened candlelight. 'M'sieur le Lieutenant', the only other French officer in the Company was about my age, but he knew a damn sight more about soldiering than I did. I felt this again later in Austria when a battalion of

Waffen SS surrendered to my company and I met the eyes of a lieutenant wearing the *Ritterkreuz*.

The captain of the Goums, a fine-looking man of about twenty-five, radiated courtesy, puffing at his cigarette and conversing with Jimmy. As a boy I had trodden the snows of Smolensk with Marshal Ney and swept along with Murat's glittering squadrons; in my ears had echoed the *pas de charge* of the Old Guard, and I saw with envy that both wore the crested, embossed helmets of the French Army, the Adrian. They might be manning American machine-guns and on their equipment US might be stamped, but the gleam of those helmets in candlelight belonged to Verdun and St Cyr.

Le Capitaine had a small matter to dispose of before he left, he added casually; two Germans in disguise had wandered into his outposts and he would shoot them before he left. 'Ah, yes, they were *les Boche* alright ... they had unfamiliar grenades on their belts ... a small matter, no need to worry us, perhaps we would like a cognac', producing a bottle of the stuff. Jimmy looked a bit startled at this news and, after a rapid flow of French and a courteous wave by our host, told me to go and look at these 'Germans'.

With the lieutenant as guide, I went to the rampart and there surrounded by trigger-fingering Goums found two lost and scared waifs from the Rifles. Lost and detached from their company, up on the left, they had blundered into the Barbary corsairs who took one look at the 2-inch mortar-bombs in their pouches which they did not recognise, and passed immediate sentence of death. As soon as the two spoke I knew they were on our side but, to satisfy the grim circle around them, asked who their colonel was. When one blurted out in a hoarse whisper 'Flash Harry' I was able to assure the execution squad that it was all 'un grand mistake' and they were 'soldats Anglais – mais oui, vraiment' and to their own vast relief took them back to Jimmy down the gully.

The next night the battalion came in and when County Kerry met Morocco confusion became rampant. My two guns up the gully and two more on Observatory Ridge were no great problem and after some hours of sweat and mule-bashing the crews had settled into their rocky holes and with heads under ground-sheets risked a fag in rotation. In between the two sections was 'Smoky Joe's', a cellar in an outhouse of the Faughs' BHQ farm or what was left of it. I had left Johnny Bowley to take over 'Smoky Joe's' with the spare gun numbers, Boswell, my batman, and various signallers. When I found him squatting beside the track and looking peevish, my temper shortened. To a grumpy 'For Christ's sake, get inside', he merely jerked his thumb at the sandbagged entry-hole and looked to Heaven for support. Into the hole I plunged, pushed aside a tattered blanket and saw the ante-room of Hell. At least thirty Goums were jammed in the dugout and a solitary lamp made of a fifty cigarette tin with a rag wick smoked in the middle. Thin upcurled beards, Attila moustaches and eagle beaks of noses filled the shadows, implacable eyes stared at nothing and the air reeked with saltpetre tobacco and human excrement. I coughed, blinked and beat a retreat to join Johnny on the rock outside. 'Get the bloody lot of us killed will those fucking savages' and Johnny was not far wrong as the false dawn showed in the east and sleepy German artillery officers polished their Zeiss lenses for another day's deal in death.

Then a French officer, with mules, appeared from nowhere. Orders, at first muttered, then snarled in some Arabic *patois* emptied 'Smoky Joe's' and all around in minutes. A stream of mules, one Goum on top and one holding the stirrup leather began to descend the hill at breakneck speed. The Frenchman stood by a rough pony held by a Goum and speeded the column on with blows from a whip which fell on man and beast as he urged them on. I warmed to him as I saw the weight of his whip cutting into those cunning, insolent and indispensable bastards who existed only to bite, kick, or crush me against walls. As the last clattered past him he swung up into the saddle and made a medieval picture with his casque against the paling stars. He looked at me standing by, leaned from his saddle and passed down his whip. 'A souvenir of the French Army, M'sieur – Bonne chance', then, orderly hanging on his stirrup, with a wave he was gone. I treasured that vicious whip, made from a bull's pizzle, for months and still hate the man who stole it from a club in Salerno.

The Invincible 'Sir Henry' (Author)

Chapter 13

Father Daniel, MC

The soldiers of 78th Division were sent in to hold positions in the mountains around Monte Cassino. Colin Gunner describes the conditions in which they lived and the courage of a Kerryborn priest, Father Dan Kelleher, in rescuing wounded under shellfire.

SANGAR LIFE engulfed us now. No digging down six feet into the sandy soil of Capua – laborious piling of rock with a pathetic little roof took place on those adamantine slopes. Where were you now Corporal Boyce with your tales of the Waziris and Khyber, from those long ago marches in the Algerian heat? These were no Pathans or Afridis facing us here. This enemy dealt not in the single brain-splashing shot of the rifle, but in generalised and wholesale death. No need to view Dead Mule corner for proof; by day and night the stench was eloquent testimony to their efficiency. Many alarms there were during that three weeks when we crouched and lay in these shelters; no excursions save for the odd, in every sense, one, of the battle patrol. We were many times better off than the battalion directly facing the Monastery, where throwing the contents of his lavatory tin out of the back of his sangar, earned for many a man a hail of mortar bombs. Just try sharing a rock hole about the size of two coffins with three others, then , in a prone position, lower your costume and fill a small tin held in the hand. The stink of excrement competed with the death smell on every position. Bowels will not wait for nightfall. Down below in the town matters were similar and here we heard of stretcher bearers of both sides meeting for a friendly chat, but I never did get confirmation of that German Major who asked a stretcher party if they had any Players cigarettes.

If the previous battles had proved beyond doubt or cavil that the German Parachute Division had a resolution and courage in defence of their terrible Thermopylae that evoked the admiration of the world and drew from Field Marshal Alexander the comment: 'What men', then their behaviour during those weeks of static war increased that admiration tenfold. Travel where you wish along that blood and ordure-smeared limbo that ran from Tavernelle to San Angelo, the rimless helmets of Heilmann's paratroopers gleamed through the fog and smoke, a living symbol of martial valour. Literally they were faithful unto death.

Boredom was an enemy, until something happened, so much so that it was said that a rather senior officer when asked what kept him so busy with his pencil replied, 'I am writing to Shirley Temple'. Until something happened, like the howl and roar that nearly moved 'Smoky Joe's' off the map one afternoon when beams fell in and the shells set fire to an old dump of grenades or like the tall figure in the dark who rose up behind me on Observatory Ridge and Major Larry Collis nearly gave me a burst of his Tommy-gun in the back.

And the night that Cairo village received Evensong from the German guns and while every living soul in that heaving rubble lay flat and prayed, a figure walked calmly among the shellbursts carrying a dying man in his arms to shelter. No-one grudged Father Daniel Kelleher, The Kerryman, that MC and he probably got a ghostly pat on the shoulder from old Saint Benedict himself, peering from Heaven to see what we were making of all his architecture. The Church Militant or Triumphant? – who can say?

Apart from the bad character getting boils and departing grinning on a mule, No 7 had had no casualties by the time the Poles turned up again to relieve us. As we met again in the dark and helped them to stumble and curse their way into their/our homes, for homes they were now, we did not know that this was to be the scene of Poland's glory and the last home for almost all who took over our positions.

Leaving behind our Vickers guns for them I conducted one to our rampart in the gully and laying his hands on the breech in the darkness hissed in our common schoolboy French: 'Ici la mitrailleuse'. Fortunately I heard the rattle of his matchbox as he pulled it out to have a better look and was in time to inform him that the white house fifty yards away was occupied by watchful Germans. All the darkness in the world may not put out one candle, but one stick grenade would certainly have put out his match.

As we started to slog back over the valley, Teddy Cullen, the company commander, told me that I was to go on leave to Amalfi, which cheered me immensely. By five in the morning, I had almost forgotten it as I helped Johnny Bowley push the dead weary platoon over the tailboard of a three-tonner. As they got in, they sat or lay and were instantly asleep. A lone figure in the dark still stood as I went to board the truck myself. No movement came in reply to my exasperated 'Get in the bloody truck or you can walk back', so seizing him by the belt and collar I nearly heaved a major of the New Zealand tanks in among the sleeping bodies of No 7.

Chapter 14

The Scent of Victory

After a spell out of the line to rest and train 78th Division was launched in the final offensive against the Gustav Line in May 1944. The Irish Brigade led the way in the divisional assault and succeeded in breaking through in the Liri valley to dominate Highway 6, the main road to Rome, thus forcing the German paras to pull out of Monte Cassino. The advance to Rome followed, with more fighting for the Brigade as May came to an end.

AMALFI WAS living proof that Heaven existed. At last I saw the Bay of Naples, Capri and Pompeii; at last I heard 'Come Back to Sorrento' in its real setting. And, as a bonus, I saw the blessing of the boats when the fishing fleet came in, flares pooling the flat water, the bell of Amalfi Cathedral tolling and the chants of response rising up to the Villa Cappucini. I gawped with all the rest when the gorgeous red-haired Countess drove in her smart pony and trap down the waterfront, and agreed that the Count knew his business when it came to picking his home and wife.

Together with Jack Simmons of the Buffs, I broke the bank on lobster suppers in the correctly named *Bucha Di Bacchus* and was reported by some buffoon of a base colonel for disorderly behaviour in the bar: who did he report me to? And it was with Jack that I toured the Villa Cimbroni in Positano on a very hot day. We had an Italian guide who was desperately anxious to justify the large fee we had paid him in our fog of hangovers. After about an hour of this culture session we both had only one desire,the bougainvillaea-hung terrace of a cool bar looking down on the blue and white of the rocks below. Rather than cause him to burst into tears I followed our guide up some lizard-strewn, herb-scented track while Jack muttered and grumbled. The guide paused and, with the air of a man who had done his duty, pointed to some ordinary looking villa half-hidden in the trees and boomed: 'And there, gentlemen, is where Greta Garbo slept with Leopold Stokowski'.

Back at Caiazzo where I rejoined the Company it was only lacking the sea. We waited in a lovely long green valley as the days lengthened and grew warmer, and nobody had any doubts as to where we were going next.

In best *'Tell 'em everything'* tradition all were soon squatting on the long warm grass in front of a blackboard where arrows and shadings depicted the next, and hopefully, last battle of Cassino. Only three facts commanded real

The Author, wearing 'that cap' (Author)

attention. Our Division was to break out of a bridgehead near the town, swing right, and cut the road behind Cassino; the Poles were to take the Monastery (mutters of 'good luck to them') and ten thousand Goums were to be 'turned loose' near Monte Maio.

With David Davison, I walked back to the Company, both of us with our own thoughts, thoughts soon dispelled by the sight of Johnny Bowley pushing and bossing No 7 Platoon into a grinning little group behind two mounted Vickers guns while an Italian photographer dived in and out of his black cape and juggled his pan of gunpowder. It would be alright; we were all together and we had come a long way.

I have vowed since the beginning of this story that when it came to the Battle of Cassino the name of John Horsfall would stand in the first line. There it is, and let it stand. But what was Cassino? The Verdun of the Second World War; the hour when the Germans could still have won; the jaws that consumed divisions; the Calvary of New Zealand; the Golgotha of the German parachutists; the Pass of Roncesvalles; the Gateway to Rome? A place or a time?? Or was it perhaps where the last gleam of glory caught the helmets of the last romantic army – the often changing band of brothers who had marched from Katmandu, Warsaw, Cairo, Wexford, Auckland and Algiers so many miles to this summit of war; this sternest, hardest battle of all? *'As you nightly pitched your moving tents a day's march nearer home'*. I make no withdrawal of that word *romantic*, for those who fought and fell in those splendid sunny days of that Italian spring did so, as the war correspondent Christopher Buckley said, in a setting that was 'theatrical and noble'. *Rubbish* cry the realists; just as well cough your life out in an industrial slum gutter as under the peaks of the Apennines on the roads that lead to the Eternal City. It's a bullet or a splinter just the same. But battle is theatre raised to the last degree and the Angel of Death has a nobility to those who live with him daily and to whom he often comes as a friend whether under the sun of Austerlitz, the shadow of the Pyramids or the far-off spires and cupolas of St Peter's.

Only those with the soul of a dried olive would deny a sweat-drenched, terrified rifleman that consolation as he put his hand into the hand of God and crossed the Rapido that May night, while the sky sheeted white and danced and two thousand guns erupted from Monte Cairo to the Tyrrhenian Sea. After so long with the Faughs, No 7 was allocated this time to the Rifles, but we were pretty ecumenical about that sort of thing. Just as long as they had the green shamrock on their arm it was all one to us, although every time we went back to a battalion it seemed to be a new one. But before joining the Rifles the crossing had to be made. The 4th Division had done the assault across the river and secured a shallow bridgehead; as we moved down to the river it was their bodies that littered the approaches to the Congo bridge. Even the smoke cloud, kept going night and day to screen the bridge from the Monastery, did not screen a company of the King's Liverpool who were shelled to ribbons before they even crossed the river.

I heard a voice call 'Hello, Colin' as we neared the crossing and saw a familiar face in a file of Hampshires; an old friend with whom I had bathed and marched many times in Algeria. To my amazed look at his private soldier's tunic and the Bren on his shoulder he grinned: 'Oh, a little difference of opinion recently – I'll tell you all about it some time'. The carrier drew away from the file and left me wondering and guessing. But I know it was with all his wonderful self-assurance and light-heartedness that he fell next day in the attack and I never wanted to know details of the 'little difference'.

Waved on by worn-out sappers we did not linger but bumped across the Bailey into the sunken lane and open field to find the Rifles' battalion. Even as the carriers made what cover they could the tracks set off dozens of those foul foot-removers, the Schu-mine. Of all inventors of war gadgets, the creator of the Schu-mine was surely the only one whom every infantry soldier could have watched with pleasure as he perished by inches, preferably mutilated in leg and testicles by one of his own brainchildren. Artillery was feared, Spandau bursts hated, mortars dreaded, but the Schu-mine inspired sick horror in the infantry. They unmanned us in both the psychological and physical senses.

But it was the fireflies of the Piopetto stream that remain in the memory, for the attack was delayed till the next morning and in the anxious dusk as the Rifles' officers met and conferred the fireflies glowed and twinkled away as if all the dust, noise and gunfire had inspired them to add to the lethal flickers and flashes now visible everywhere along the front: at least they weren't noisy.

The Skins led the way up Death Valley at dawn and it was a measure of the battle's ferocity that the battalion bounds were measured only in hundreds of yards. I kept the overlay map of Cassino well-hidden, even from Johnny Bowley, as it was simply a black mass of marked and known German positions. Teddy Cullen and I were sitting in a jeep that morning and scrambled out to touch our caps to Major John Horsfall, second-in-command of the Rifles, as he strolled among the Support Company. The guns going hard behind us suddenly seemed to go mad as they flooded overhead in a howling crescendo and the Skins' assault company got across the road at the head of the valley. While Major Horsfall chatted to Teddy, a runner came panting up and blurted out to him that Colonel Goff of the Rifles was dead. With just that as a guide he politely bade us good-day and went with the runner to take command of his battalion.

All was activity, for the Rifles were next to attack, over the road towards a not yet glimpsed Casa Sinagoga. Teddy pushed off with No 6 Platoon to go with the Skins while I sought Charles Bird of the Rifles, who was already getting his carriers on the move. Shouting to Johnny to follow on, I jumped in with Jack Tuff and tagged on to the back of the Rifles. The halt was called halfway up Death Valley while the Rifles got into line on the road ready for going over the top. Tanks, carriers, jeeps, the Rifles filing forward, the Skins' wounded coming back, prisoners, all filled the valley. And knowing a good target when they saw it the Germans pumped artillery and mortar fire in as hard as they could.

As soon as a halt was called No 7 leaped for cover and there was no need to urge them to scrape shallow holes beside or under the carriers. Over the little hillock at the valley's entry, the scene of a Hampshire VC, the sky suddenly blackened as salvoes of shrapnel crashed overhead with surprisingly little result. A returning tank carried a load of dead and dying past, the front dripping like a butcher's shop, the driver staring dead ahead, while nearby Teddy and No 6 caught it full blast from mortarfire. Kanharn lay dead across the track, Sergeant Hebbard died when the stretcher party got to him, while three more were wounded and a voice cried from a burning carrier: 'Shoot me, Paddy – for Christ's sake, shoot me'. The hatch of a Sherman flew open and a perspiring Lancer remarked to a passing file of the Rifles: 'God, these mortars scare the shit out of me' to be asked in turn by a rifleman armoured with a khaki shirt: 'and what in the name of Jesus do you think they do to me then?'

I lay beside the carrier and saw the shellbursts just ahead by the road, and prisoners literally sprinting with laden stretchers in the smoke. A shell skimmed the carrier and burst behind among Johnny and his crew and out of the dust and smoke came those cries that pierced one's soul. Johnny was shaken but unhurt; by a miracle so were the other three, but Boswell, patient, placid, ever-willing Boswell, was shell-shocked into oblivion; unhurt and unmarked, save where no field dressing or rum could help him, no comrade could bring a word of comfort or cheer. He was beyond our voices now as we detailed someone to lead him back along the valley. These were the saddest cases of all, that sudden slamming of a shell that finally smashed the nerves screwed down to explosion of one who knew that the breaking-point was near, yet did not and could not say 'I can't go on'. It was, I think, the greatest bravery of all, fighting that bottled demon knowing that some day someone would pull out the cork.

The attack companies had gone over the top now and Charles Bird, helmet

May 1945. A Guard of Honour of the Faughs presents arms as a Russian Corps Commander arrives at 5 (British) Corps HQ at Wolfsburg (IWM)

well over his eyes, waved us to follow. Even the valley with its dust, death and explosions, seemed preferable to showing heads over the road, but up and over the road we went with not the faintest idea of what would meet us. A track led straight on and at the end was the battered and burning Casa Sinagoga. Many fountains shot up in the plough and in the ditches as every driver gave his carrier full throttle and I shouted to Jack Tuff to speed it up as one large geyser shot up beside the road: I had great faith in the ability of the German gunners to hit roads and tracks, especially straight ones.

Into Sinagoga we all piled and Charles told me to get two of the Vickers and follow him. He had already spoken to Major Horsfall in the farm. Unloading two of the guns we carried them down a cornfield to the leading company in another building and despite their loads the crews covered the ground with some speed, as the Spandau fire swished in the cornstalks. One gun was set up in a window and one below in the yard: a quick word with the Rifles' officer and we were off to get the other two guns into position. Halfway back, by a stationary Sherman, we heard the screech and moan of *Nebelwerfers* on their way – and on their way to us. No shelter here but under the tank and both of us dived and burrowed between the warm earth and warmer tank exhausts. The first salvo burst all around us and as we heard the second on its way the tank started up its engine. Charles's eyes met mine with total consternation; out of the *Nebels* to be squashed like a cockroach! Charles looked calmly up at the steel belly and intoned 'Don't move now for God's sake – there's a good fellow'. And the Sherman did not move while the next salvo landed and, almost before the last one arrived roaring like a train, we crawled out, shaken and unsquashed.

At Sinagoga we found one of the Vickers guns flattened but the crew had been saved by their trench as a Lancers' tank had moved back over crew and gun.

Sinagoga quietened down a little and Charles Bird occupied a fine German dugout by the hayricks. Before disappearing into the depths he remarked 'Should you want me, my standard will indicate if I am in residence' and placed his scarf on a broken rifle. I found the winestore but shellfire had been there first as the smashed barrels and broken roof showed. The cellar was out of bounds, chock full with wounded – both ours and German – and a German medical captain earned ten Iron Crosses as he toiled away and shell-dressings were passed down to him in the dark. But the sun seemed nailed in the sky and I found myself muttering with many others 'Oh God, please let that sun go down – Oh God, hurry up the dark please'. Soldiers' prayers are always short and elemental; whatever they lacked in style they more than made up for in fervour. There was something very basic and blunt in the favourite 'Oh God, let me get through today (or tonight) and I'll try to be better tomorrow', as the mutterer tried with all his heart to storm the ear of Heaven. And who shall say their pathetic plea was not heard louder then those anthems 'pealing in fretted vaults'.

But go down the sun would not; it shone on strongly in the smoke and dust haze while the ridge near us burst into flames as the Rifle Brigade came up on the left. Somewhere, someone shouted – 'Look at the Monastery – the Polish flag is on the Monastery' and field glasses were swung to the right and upwards to see faintly in the blur and over the jagged outline the black eagle of Poland perched on the battlements. How fitting, how very fitting it all was that no garbled whistles and squeaks on radios should let the world know that at long last the rusty, immovable hinge had been battered open, and that in all those desperate hours on Phantom Ridge, 593 and Albanate some Pole had carried his country's colour with him to hoist it gloriously above the smoking, thundering battleline below. It did not bring any dramatic hush on our front for, as night eventually did fall, I found No 7 now only mustered two guns and crews and had had two guns destroyed and six men wounded.

With the two remaining guns I went a little further with Major Mervyn Davies and his E Company and while Mervyn and his sergeant-major se-lected a deep concrete dugout as their HQ, the sergeant-major in the light of his match woke figures snoring on the bunks and informed two very tired Germans that they were prisoners. They did not seem very surprised and went sleepily back with an escort.

The Skins at dawn stormed the key village of Piumerola. What was left of No 7 Platoon and I were sent with them and went in with their reserve company just as their waving, smiling, very bloodstained Colonel Bredin went back to hospital. Wounded as the attack started, no power or pain would shift him and he remained propped against a jeep, and held by his orderly, until his companies had gained the village. Then, and only then, he departed. Of three colonels, the score now read: one dead; one wounded. But if less dramatic than the Polish standard on the Monastery, that assault by the battered, depleted Skins had unlocked the gate on our front. For coming out of Piumerola was a column of prisoners; for the first time they were prisoners from the parachute division, those stark, Krupp-hard professionals who had stood so long and fought so well. There were nearly a hundred of them, in fearsome dappled jumping-jackets and pot-shaped helmets. This was the scent of victory at last, visible in that grim column.

No 7 stopped by a place marked on that sinister map in my back pocket as 'The Barracks' and it was along its long wall that I ventured with three of the gun-crew, sublimely confident that the Skins had cleared the way for us.

Turning into a broken doorway I crashed into reverse. A German sat at a table just inside with his back towards me. The Street Fighting Manual lays down that a grenade should be tossed in and then followed up in such situations, but our little group of course had no grenades so I risked a cautious peep. He still sat there and, entering, I shook his shoulder as he sat, head pillowed on his arms as if fast asleep. He was a German parachute lieutenant and he rolled slowly off the chair onto the floor as I stared open-mouthed. A mortar bomb had burst in the door behind him, killing him instantly but, for some freak reason, not blowing him off his chair. His quickly-pocketed Luger and field-glasses were on the table beside a smashed radio; still discussing this strange death we were chased out of Piumerola and sent back to the Rifles, attacking over to the right to cut the road. It was all over when we got there and all I had to do was to install the two guns in a farm to cover the road. Major Horsfall joined us there and told me to accompany him back to the other company down a rustic little track. He showed no sign that in forty-eight hours he had assumed command of his battalion and carried it forward victoriously into its greatest battle, but looked more as if he were back in his native Warwickshire strolling down a lane for a day among the partridges.

When the *Nebels* let out their elephant trumpet in front I needed no prompting. Into the leaf mould and brambles of the ditch I shot with polished skill. As the moans and squeals filled the air I ventured an upward glance to meet his amused smile. 'Aiming at the road, I think,' was his accurate prediction as, leaning on his stick, he watched their descent. 'Ah, yes sir, of course,' was the only reply but it was with red neck and face that I clambered out and trotted on with him.

I joined a corporal of the Faughs next day who was pissing on an abandoned and still loaded *Nebelwerfer* and agreed with him that it was something we had both wanted to do for a long time.

Aquino fell just in front and at long last the carrier tracks ground into the Via Casilina on the road to Rome. But only for about a mile until we turned into a wood and waited for the Guards to clear some Germans from Monte Piccolo. We spent the night in that wood and were shelled by a veritable Belial of cannon; a leviathan that dug craters deep enough to swallow a tank and only stopped at dawn with everyone in a nerve-shattered state. So shattered were we that no-one appreciated the joke at a track junction where a Canadian Irish soldier stood chanting monotonously: 'Canadian Irish to the left, English Irish to the right'. But right or left it did not matter, the hinge was forced, the door lay flat and we had crossed the threshold to the first capital city of Europe.

Chapter 15

The Green Plume

Rome fell on June 4th, 1944, two days before the Allies landed in France on D Day. From Rome the attacking armies chased the Germans northwards to Lake Trasimene where there was a fierce encounter in which the Irish Brigade was heavily involved. After the battle 78th Division was pulled back and sent to Egypt for rest and training. At the same time Colin Gunner received his transfer to the Faughs.

GOING TO the Rifles HQ the next day for orders, I knew that there would be no flower-strewn, vino-drinking jaunt to Rome, for passing the Faughs BHQ many blanket-wrapped bodies outside showed that at least one 88 crew had obeyed their orders to 'shoot and scoot' to some effect before beating it back north. At the Rifles' Orders Group, things were also somewhat chilly when the Intelligence Officer supplied his colonel with a map of the Balkans instead of the approaches to the Tiber. The air froze solid while this boob was rectified and I kept my eyes riveted on a rum-jar under the Quartermaster's seat.

But by next evening we had parted from the Rifles and groped our way in the dark to join up with our own company once again. We stopped on one little rise and watched for half an hour the constant glow in the sky as bridge after bridge was blown ahead of us and listened above the whirr of the cicadas for the low distant thud. I gave up after midnight and called a halt in a small village. At first light on June 6th, 1944, as our distant cousins were splashing ashore in Normandy, we found the road and the rendezvous.

It was here that we heard of D Day, but I was not very interested, for on arriving I had tried my hand once again on a motorbike and broadsiding round a dusty corner found an oncoming tank in the way. The bike was squashed under his tracks while I rolled once more ditchwards and collected a face full of thorns.

Teddy Cullen gave me the news, and said that the bike could truthfully be written off as having sustained a direct hit. The only reaction to D Day from the Platoon was 'About time too, now where's the breakfast?' A late start meant a late arrival on the outskirts of the city and it was past midnight before we crossed the Tiber and headed north again. Our platoon intellectual proved a mine of knowledge but lost considerable prestige when he assured his crew,

with a wave of the curly-stemmed pipe, that the brand new sports stadium
built by Mussolini was the Colosseum. But it was a moonlit night on that
bridge and I had no difficulty in recalling the lines of 'Tiber, Father Tiber to
whom the Romans pray.'

Our muddy hillside where we halted and waited for two days was without
significance save for the caves, reputed to have been Kesselring's HQ. But
the souvenir hunters retired baffled as every cave was on fire and explosions
within daunted even Sergeant Taylor, that prince of looters. Nearby, a battery
of monster American guns were in action with ponderous roars. I watched
intrigued as the American gun-number who fired the brute tended a still,
complete with copper spiral. He was cooking vino and catching the distillate
in a mess-tin. When the squawk-box summoned him to duty he sprinted to the
firing lanyard, yelled 'Rommel, count yuh men' and pulled before flashing
back to catch the precious drip. Johnny Bowley suggested that the brew
would fire the gun better than any cordite but was not offered a sample.

I wandered down the hillside and saw a long-forgotten face sitting by my
bivouac – Lotty, Louis Lottenburg, who had shared those extra drills on the
windy barrack yard at York. He was now a platoon commander in the East
Surreys and passing through on the advance. We only had time for a mug of
tea before he had to leave. Next day he was in action in street-fighting and his
road from York ended with a sniper's bullet.

Viterbo and Orvieto came and went before we heard that the Faughs were
ahead, and as a bonus for a sharp little action, had won a real castle complete
with picture gallery, feather-beds and a billiard saloon. Billiards is associated
with green baize and it was noticed that many had very new, neatly-sewn,
green shamrocks on their arms later. As for picture galleries, Dick Unwin, a
large blond patrol expert in D Company, became very aggressive if the
subject was raised and razor-blades mentioned.

From this eyrie of a castle red-banded hats surveyed the shimmer of Lake
Trasimene before them and, thumbing their Staff College Manuals at the page
marked Hannibal, launched the Rifles and the Skins along its shore. Again,
No 7 drew the Skins in the Irish Sweep, but the Lancashire Fusiliers already
down on the lake sent warning rumbles back; rumbles of the familiar story of
the hastily improvised German battle-group fighting with the old murderous
precision. Not only fighting but hitting back hard as we found in Pucciarelli,
where we spent a hectic day with a Skins' company and a troop of Canadian
tanks trying to stop a counter-attack between ourselves and the Rifles in San
Fatucchio. The Rifles, with their six-pounders blasting away in the streets and
led by the victor of Sinagoga, John Horsfall, had won another brilliant
victory. Their RSM, Girvan, won the MC as he entered the fray with the

assault artillery. An officer crawled along the low cemetery wall before rising to scramble over it, as a similarly crawling German did the same at precisely the same spot; the Rifles officer fired first. Dick Gray of the mortars set up his spy-glass in the campanile bell-tower, but was then chased down the spiral staircase by a Panther tank that drilled holes in the tower as Dick shot down the steps on his backside, just beating the tank's gunner by ten feet. One O Group of the Faughs was dispersed by a flying cupboard when the wall came in on the planners and their plots.

On a smaller scale we received the same attention. After a shell and mortar bombardment of Cassino quality, the houses at the top of the village were lost and unfriendly noises came from the orchards behind us. In one of the houses, Teddy Cullen and 6 Platoon found that the ground floor no longer held 'Alderman Joseph O'Toole' and his band of Skins, but Germans who proceeded to empty their Schmeissers up into the ceiling. Dismounting a Vickers gun from its tripod, Teddy used it in road-drill fashion to fire downwards and try to evict his attackers; MacAlpine's Construction Company would have been proud of him. A well-meaning corporal, spotting Germans below the window, heaved a grenade out and achieved a perfect rebound on a springy tree branch. MacAlpine and company hit the floor as it went off – without casualties.

The Canadian tanks saved the day by pumping HE shells into the lost houses and killing most of the attack group. Down the street I was picking myself off a heap of rubble in a ruined house after a mortar-bomb landed and moved me through a door without opening it. With another, I carried in Private Paul from the orchard where he had been shot through the head and placed his body in a stable. Returning to the orchard I sprayed away with my captured Schmeisser in the general direction of the now clear shouts in German, while Johnny and the guns fired from the windows. On ducking back I found the muzzle of a Sherman's 75mm in my face; the Canadian tank commander made it clear in vivid terms that, if I continued to use a distinctive sounding German automatic, he would not be to blame if he blew my 'ass off'. I took the hint and carried a rifle for the rest of the day.

The counter-attack died away but the shelling increased, driving us down into a convenient cellar. And in there we squatted while the tumult outside rose and fell. Joined by a Canadian tank sergeant, we lent him a pick as he tapped the walls speculatively. Sure enough a few blows showed the false wall and making an entry hole he dived in and emerged with a large sack of sugar. 'Thanks boys, the rest is yours' and he went up the steps lugging his sack. This was too much; hoist with our own petard. I was first in the hole and in the match-flare saw the rows of bottles neatly racked up. No time for finesse now: off with the first cork and up with the bottle and down to my bowels shot the plug of rancid black olive oil floating on the top. When I had finished vomiting and retching I helped load up the carriers with our treasure trove during a lull in the bombardment.

The shelling was the German signal to pull back, for darkness brought the calm. A fiery dark it was, however, for buildings blazed in both village and along the front. In the gleam of the fires I met the imperturbable Charles Gladitz of the Skins, carrying a bundle under his arm. He greeted me with: 'Where in Hell have all the washerwomen gone? I haven't changed my shirt for a week'. I pointed out that it was hardly likely that any washerwomen had remained to ply their trade in Pucciarelli or San Fatucchio while the battle raged, but he was unconvinced, remarking: 'Well, there must be one some-where'. Pausing, he nodded towards a burning farm on the right and confided: 'I'll tell you something, there aren't any down there. It's chockfull of angry men – they just shot at me'. He disappeared into the night, singleminded in his search for hygiene.

Under a 1914–18 style rolling barrage the Faughs stormed forward next day and No 7 was allotted an abandoned railway train for a target as it was suspected that a German position was beneath it. It was a small boy's dream to see belt after belt crashing into the locomotive and shattering the coal on the tender, but orders came to pull out. For a week or so it had been firmly believed that the whole Division was going back to the UK for the second front and I had been assured by the quartermaster-sergeant that he knew someone who had actually seen the movement order. He probably had, but somehow had misread Egypt as UK. But to the orders to pull out and rejoin the company was added the footnote: 'Lieutenant Gunner not to accompany Platoon. Report to CO, 1st Royal Irish Fusiliers at once'. My transfer had arrived but although requested and expected it was still a shock to see No 7 climb aboard their carriers and leave me at the roadside after all those miles from Algiers.

Johnny Bowley and I shook hands and muttered banalities. I watched his figure, now more to me than any brother, vanish in the dust with a wave, my mind awash with a flood of emotional memories – 'Cheerio, Johnny – Look after yourself, Skipper'. Another die was cast since I wrote that 'Any Infantry Regiment of the line' on the proforma and deep down I felt this was the last and most dangerous throw of all. In the jeep heading to the Faughs I schemed of how I could still get the best of both worlds. Was I not a trained machine-gunner, and did they not have a machine-gun platoon in their support com-pany? Obviously such talents as mine would not be squandered in a rifle company. That was it of course. I would, at last, be a full member of the Old

Faughs and wear their arrogant green plume; at last their badge of glory would shine in my cap, the scream of their pipes and bugles would be my music, but still I would not be in much more danger than before. One of them at last, but not of those rifle companies about whose turnover of personnel it made me dizzy to think.

I remembered that their colonel, Jim Dunnill, had been captured the day before in the attack on Ranciano. He had completed the trinity of the colonels who led their battalions into the Cassino attack: one dead; one wounded; one missing. I also knew that their majors had all become casualties over the last few weeks so I was not totally unprepared when, opening the door in the HQ farmhouse, I saw behind a table their Adjutant, Brian Clark, with a major's crowns on his shoulders.

Command of the battalion had not mellowed him, for it was with an adjutant's glacial stare that he met my salute and it was with an Adjutant's voice that he shattered my little plans. 'So you've arrived at last. You will go to A Company' A Company was very much a rifle company. Still not believing my ears, and doubting his sanity, I walked down the path to a little line of bivouacs on the slope. Fusiliers lying out in the sun looked at me curiously and I felt very lonely and timid when I asked a tall sergeant-major where I would find A Company. His eyes were the first friendly ones I met as he looked down with a mixture of enquiry and amusement. 'A Company, sir? This is A Company, I'm the CSM'. I was there at last, the wanderings were over, the doubts resolved. Whatever the future held now, I had come home.

When CSM Storey sang '*Galway Bay*' that night at a sergeants' party in the company lines, the tears rolled down his cheeks. Only too grateful at being invited, although such a newcomer, I concentrated on the drink and song until a hand of iron gripped my shoulder and A Company's CSM, now smiling broadly, bellowed across the tobacco haze: 'You'll be alright, my son, I'll look after you'. Like all his promises, or threats, he kept it all too well and Shipp, the writer of Wellington's Peninsular War, never spoke a truer word than when he said he knew 'no finer campaigning comrades than the Old Faughs'. The Old Faughs of our Peninsular War knew no finer than CSM 'Big Fred' Taylor, an Irish soldier and gentleman.

To our surprise when we camped at Tivoli outside Rome, Father Dan, the regimental priest, had not posted the Pope and assumed the Chair of Peter. He had, however, re-organised the Irish College and arranged an audience with His Holiness for the Irish Brigade. But first a select band of Catholic *left-footers* were taken in privately, leaving the stout sons of Ulster muttering about *Old Red Socks* and whistling *The Boyne Water*. I could be very neutral and detached on this subject but noted that the pipes always seemed to play

The Sash immediately after *The Wearing of the Green* despite any convictions of the Pipe Major. All went in the best spirit in the end and with the others I stood by the dais in the great Throne Room when the small, white figure was carried in on the *sedilia*, and gave his blessing impartially to the pious and the Protestant. *'Our heart rejoices to see the sons of St Patrick once more among us'*. Diffidently at the back, watching the genuflections and ring-kissing my neutrality moved, then lurched towards my left foot. It was not just the splendour of the Noble Guard, the setting of the magnificence contrasting with the plain, pale little man with the piercing eyes behind those army issue specs; not just the jumble in the mind – *'Tu es Petros; the keys of the Kingdom; Bernini, Michelangelo; the Fisherman'* – *but an awe, thinking that down all these centuries through war, invasion, revolution, fire and hate, through bad men and saints, had come this frail holder of a title that rang in my brain like the bells of his parish; 'Christ's Vicar on Earth'*. I knew many of that audience whom I would classify as hard men; I knew none who was unmoved. As for Father Dan at the elbow, I expected to see a Red Hat clapped on his head as Brigadier Scott called for 'Three Cheers for His Holiness'.

It was as well that the audience was held that day and not after the Ball that night given by the Irish Brigade in the Barbarini Palace. Next morning only jagged impressions stabbed the splitting heads: drums in the courtyard; pipes under the painted ceilings; colliding lines in Irish jigs; the roar of *Killaloe* and Dick Doyle of C Company doing very well with the pretty daughter of the Irish Minister. To put a damper on the holiness and hilarity the battalion loaded on the traditional *8 horses; 40 men* cattle-trucks to go south to Taranto and Egypt and perhaps purgatory consists of several million miles of that form of travel.

Father Dan did the greatest penance as he was suffering from dysentery. Attempts to hang rearwards out of the door were stopped after several close shaves with signal posts and his often-emptied margarine tin was not nearly large enough. Poor Dan's face only brightened once when, halted in the ruins of Cassino, shouts of 'Dan, Father Dan, look here, Dan' came from the engine. He answered the calls and looked out of the door. A smile lit his drawn and ill face when he saw, flying from the engine, a green, white and red Italian flag with orange substituted for the red. A brief halt, a rush to secure vino, a pilfered and quickly-altered flag, an instruction to the driver: 'Ah, shut your gob' and we puffed through that evil desert with the republican colours flying in the breeze. Dan raised his hand to his cap and shouted to the engine 'And it's the only one I'll ever salute' with no knowledge that one day he would be laid to rest in Berlin under the Union Flag he had served so nobly.

The camp at Taranto where we waited for the ship was hardly better than the train, hot, dusty and hated by all. But in this smelly little backwater, where I grumbled as loudly as the rest, two cheering events came to me. First of all, I had No 7 Platoon once again and took that as an omen of good fortune. The second was my first collision with Sir Henry. Collision is correct – no-one ever met Sir Henry. He has a name that does not matter; my first glimpse of his tall figure, broad shoulders, black curly hair and piratical moustaches elicited: 'Good God – Sir Henry Morgan'. He was a rifle platoon commander detested by his seniors, loathed by the Adjutant, tolerated by his equals and an object of fascination and horror to his men. He was Falstaff, Pantaloon and Brendan Behan, a living embodiment of all that Irishmen would like to forget but secretly admire. To me he was a joy and delight who, despite all failings, brought mirth in times and places where Hell itself could not be so bad if it held such laughter. Even now he rises like Frankenstein and threatens to dominate the pages.

I realised for the first time the value of this *El Dorado* when, after a sharp lecture from the colonel to all officers about keeping parties within decent limits, Sir Henry was found the very next morning by the colonel himself, sprawled on the floor of the Mess amid a welter of empty Marsala bottles. Whilst in open arrest he confirmed my hopes by telling me that 'All English-men are treacherous bastards' and that included me. He had served in the ranks of the Irish Guards in Tunisia where, according to him, only he 'and a blade of grass stood between Rommel and victory'. His arrival in the Faughs was marked by the fact that his worldly goods seemed to consist of a groundsheet and a walking-stick. He improved his lot by immediately plundering a German hospital which some idiot had told him to go and guard.

The battalion with the now-liberated and briefly disciplined Sir Henry were lifted in the *Durban Castle* to Port Said in peacetime cruise conditions, and I marvelled at one of the pipers sitting on a hatch-cover blowing jazz, flute-like, from his pipe-chanter.

By rail we went to Qassasin on the canal and lived in endless rows of tents, studded with shiny tin latrines, and ate cold collations in our dusty Mess-tent. With Dick Doyle I swam from Africa to Asia, all fifty yards of it, and with him also cursed the Adjutant for putting us on a PT course. McGee of my platoon hopped and skipped in the heat with the rest of us on this idiocy but when, during a period devoted to unarmed combat, he was asked by the athletic and non-combatant PT Instructor: 'What's the first thing you do with a prisoner', he looked up sourly from the sand and grunted: 'Pinch his fucking watch'.

Watches must have been McGee's obsession for he smartly borrowed three pounds from me after a plausible story of having to pay for his to be repaired.

I could not see a watch repairer within fifty miles, but parted with the money, only to be told by the CSM that evening that 'the crow has never had one'. 'Crow' was the CSM's definition of anyone who merited his disapproval.

Alexandria was the real Egypt at last, when we moved to Sidi Bishr just outside the city, again in tents. But the camp no longer mattered as leave to Alex and Cairo was handed out to everyone. The real Egypt, and the real *Gyppos* as we soon found out as the gharri-wallahs, procurers, bar men and small boys welcomed us with a hand in both our pockets. Despite all warnings I bought a paper at the traffic-lights and, as the jeep moved off, discovered it was a week old. Cecil Beard, the Signals Officer, treated himself to an expensive lighter and, producing it with a flourish in the Club at the lunchtime beer session, watched the top fly across the room as he snapped it open. Opening a juicy book on one stall my eyes popped at the random page and I thrust piastres into the small pink palm. With the promised treat I lay naked on the bed in the afternoon heat, and found the same pages repeated all through the book.

But a wealthy member of the battalion touched the ceiling of Egyptian cunning. A hotel was not good enough for him on his leave in Cairo and, guided by a friendly native, he inspected a luxurious apartment which just happened to be vacant for a week. He paid his deposit and departed for the Club, the front door-key jingling in his pocket. Mindful of family and beautiful fiancée at home he toured the Mouski and the shops, selecting handbags, scent and curios. Midnight, or later, found him glowing with brandy and prawns outside his apartment in a *gharri*, his parcels strewn around him. Dismounting heavily, he produced his money to pay the *jehu*, when a nightgown shot out of the alley and fled with his wallet. As he never made the athletics team at Sedbergh his short sprint in pursuit proved in vain. Puffing back he was treated to the sight of the *gharri*, full of his parcels, now driven by Ben Hur, disappearing in the middle distance. Wallet and presents gone, he inserted his latch-key and was promptly thrown out of his rented palace by a respectable Greek family. It was a touching sight to see him, back to hotel level, borrowing money from his friends the next day.

To Sir Henry, Alex meant only one thing – women. Women of any shape, size or breed; all were grinds to Sir Henry's mill. Rarely was he disappointed as his spectrum was so vast. A small setback came his way one evening when he accosted a group of us at the bar of the Cecil with the stern query: 'Have you seen that Welsh bastard?' This was taken to mean a member of the battalion well equipped physically and prominent in social activities. We *had* seen 'that Welsh bastard' and seen him with a sexy looking Armenian, but red-hot wires under the fingernails would not have made anyone admit it, as

Sir Henry spluttered 'He's got my bint' before stamping off in pursuit.

Under my mosquito net in the lines that night I heard his unsteady arrival at the Guard-tent and, after a violent argument with the taxi-driver, his rich accents ordering the Guard to 'Bayonet the black bugger's tyres', I feigned sleep as he lurched and tripped over guy ropes before entering the moonlit tent. His incantations and maledictions flowed while he rummaged in his kit and produced a Luger. With this in his hand he set off from the tent, muttering promises to blow apart people who pinched his bint. Silence fell and I went back to sleep. Walking over to the Mess for breakfast, we passed a prone figure on a little dune; Sir Henry lay peacefully sleeping, a fine film of sand had drifted over his face and his Luger muzzle still pointed purposefully at a tent as he awaited his betrayer's return.

Baited one morning at breakfast as to his sexual prowess, he confessed that the previous night he had not been up to his usual Olympian standards. His favourite place for consummation was in the bunkers of the golf course: 'Just the right angle, d'ye see'. But as the selected object of his passion that night awaited the lancers, Sir Henry's bugles suddenly blew *Retire*, or, as he put it: 'There hung me friend silent and sad – I'd overdone the brandy'.

The decorations for the Cassino battle arrived and Colonel Horsfall, commanding the battalion now, received the DSO. Many others were also on the list and the Mess celebrations were lengthy and dominated by the Brigadier, Pat Scott, who climbed the tent-pole and, squirrel-like, hung there to offer his congratulations to a cheering crowd. A rather decorous dance was given for the local Wrens from Ras el Tin naval station and I was sent with a padded three-tonner to collect a load of beauty: 'And mind you don't go drinking before you collect them'. As they gave me gin in their Mess I thought this did not apply and so accepted all that was offered, before shooting them into the Mess-tent and into the arms of my waiting and sober seniors. Duty done, I sought the bar, and heard Sir Henry comparing them unfavourably with his latest Levantine trollop, whom he had been forbidden to invite.

Despite a tantalising tale that the Division was going to the Lebanon for mountain training – and who could have trained *us* for God's sake? – it was back to Italy after these hot and happy weeks. In fitting style, I dined in the Union Grill with the others, despite having told an unco-operative manager of Barclays Bank that morning that 'it was a pity that Rommel never got to the Delta', when he refused me more money. Where the night ended I do not know, but the gangplank, the semaphore blink and the whoops of the destroyers were all too real the next morning as the sour fumes of brandy mixed horribly with the smell of paint, harbour garbage and briefly banished forebodings.

Looking quite human; that 'bloody adjutant', Brian Clark in Austria,
June 1945 (Lt Col Brian Clark)

Chapter 16

Back to Business

In September 1944 the Irish Brigade returned to Italy and went into positions in the mountains of northern Italy where they would spend another winter.

THOSE CONFIDENT predictions, always made after the fourth double of Bolonachi gin – 'it will be over before we get back'; 'they won't need us again' – faded away when we headed west once again in the *Durban Castle*. The battalion had acquired four Canadian officers now; all came to serve in what they rather grandly called *The Imperial Forces*, and one of them, the dignified Maurice Crehan, of The Irish Fusiliers of Canada, was commanding A Company. He had surprisingly displaced Jack Phelan, an experienced South African captain with an MC. No 8 Platoon had a Canadian commander, Al McLennan, of whom I knew only that he was rich and his mother, at regular intervals, sent him boxes of the most heavenly chocolates I had ever tasted: he was generous with them as well.

A different kettle of fish was Bob Hogan, from London, who although nominally a lieutenant leading a platoon, commanded more authority and respect than any other subaltern. He was much older than all the others of that rank, wore a Military Medal, and had been commissioned in the field in Africa. The air of a sergeant still clung to him, but I noticed that time and again the eyes of the old hands turned to him for confirmation of an order. As for me, I followed him blind.

Towering behind the glitter of the pips was the quiet and corrective eye of the CSM. I often wondered, but never dared to ask, what he thought as he surveyed his present leaders, what memories of his days as a young soldier and NCO must have stirred in that mind. Memories and comparisons with the real regular Sandhurst products he had known in his youth. Never once did he betray those thoughts.

I shared a tiny cabin with Al McLennan and two others on the voyage and on this trip we had taken steps to get round that noxious, Yank-orientated order about dry ships. All had brought some supplies aboard, the stony-broke majority a couple of bottles but Al was reputed to have a case of gin under his bunk. Perhaps it was this rumour that caused Father Dan to push aside the curtain just as Canada settled down after dinner to show the Limeys how to play his national game, poker.

That 'bloody adjutant' again. A youthful Brian Clark in the uniform of Captain in The Royal Irish Fusiliers.

Cards always bore me, so after losing the few shillings I had left, I clambered into my bunk to sleep. Father Dan, with a guileless 'Do you mind if I have a couple of hands?' took my place, waved graciously into the game by the ante-raising Al who was now in full cry. I dropped off and dozed under my air-blower, adjusted to hit me square in the navel but, waking at intervals, saw that although others came and went in the game the Church and Canada were the real antagonists.

The breakfast gong was sounding when I climbed down to wash and saw gleefully that Father Dan sat like Humpty Dumpty on a heap of notes and coins while the exponent of Canada's national game glumly wrote out a cheque. Dan pocketed all, and as fit and fresh as when he first sat down, strode off to his breakfast kipper. While I scraped away in the mirror, I heard an explosive colonial oath and the blood-curdling vow: 'That's the last time I ever play with a goddam priest!' Events since have confirmed my belief that seminaries run a pretty intensive course on games of chance, or perhaps the psychology of the confessional helps.

Taranto opened its drawbridge once again and we were back home. Nobody seemed to want us this time for we motored in troop-carriers back up the Adriatic coast over all the old ground, in seemingly endless fashion. At Ortona we realised how lucky we had been to be pulled out after the Sangro battle; endless rows of Canadian crosses marked that fearful Christmas they had spent inching their way into this little port on the muddy brown sea.

But it did rain, and it rained in that steady Italian fashion we knew so well. Very few were dry in those days spent homing in again on the gun flicker. Somebody at last decided they wanted us, for we turned sharp left and set off across the mountains towards Florence and the Fifth Army. Another anonymous night followed in the wet dark save for a loud Canadian voice calling 'This is not the retreat from Waterloo, Mister Gunner' when I led No 7 in a sleepy rush for a farmhouse and was called back to sleep under and around the transport.

Perhaps I was still simmering when I fell into a damp nightmare for I woke up on my feet, shouting out a warning to all around me. In my dreams I saw quite clearly that a tank had started to move and was about to run over the sleeping bodies in the dark. Through the daze of waking I slowly realised that a carrier had started its engine some fifty yards away and the subconscious had done the rest.

By night, too, we crawled over the Futa Pass and saw ahead the steady drummer flashing the sky. Business was as usual up there; Castel del Rio was the Piccadilly junction of this sector, just another dirty bedlam of a village crammed to the eaves with troops and surrounded with American gun batteries. For it was Americans we were going to relieve, those same Americans of the 88th Division whose copybook column we had admired back in the Capua days. Now the gloss had worn off those GMCs, those stateside jackets were muddy and frayed and those virgin rifle barrels were worn with cordite.

A more personal problem than battle-hardened allies was on my mind when we debussed and started to march up on relief. That most treasured of all a soldier's fleeting possessions was rebelling; I had a dose of the squits and wore that anxious expression of one who knew that to get out of marching order and into a squatting position would be a damn close-run thing. But 'Lead on, A Company' was being shouted and the files started to move up the mountain road, Maurice at the head and the CSM and myself at the rear. We had made some few miles up that slippery apology for a road, chocolate mud up to the ankles at times and the CSM in a pleasantly conversational mood, when a minor landslide in my bowels stopped me in mid-stride and with a muttered 'I'll catch you up' to the CSM, I slid down a bank towards some bush-lined mountain torrent, but even as I tore madly at belt and packstraps, nature overwhelmed me and the bottom fell out of the basement. The water of that little stream in which I sat naked from the waist down ten minutes later had a double effect, not only cleansing but paralysing in its coldness, but I was past caring. With much fingernail blowing and dancing in the mud I completed my toilet on my pocket handkerchief and averted my eyes from boots and trousers. The march of Mars on the road above me had thundered on while my internal tragedy had been played out in the bushes and a tank was passing when I regained the road. Scrambling up on the back I toasted my icy backside on its engine covers until sliding off as it drew level with the company. I was greeted by the CSM with 'as I was saying, sir . . .' and with only the slightest wrinkle of his nose he continued the conversation.

We had been on the move some fourteen hours before we clawed our way up an almost vertical bank hanging on to bushes and roots to find the foundering holes of Monte Codronco where poncho-covered GIs stood in slime and misery. Ceaselessly the sheets of rain fell from above and I could have spared myself that frozen squat in the stream as rivers ran down chest, back and legs. Thankfully the GIs dragged themselves out of their foxholes and slopped away down the bank. No 7's private real estate was a line of these holes under the rim and some more in the trees on the forward slopes of the summit. While trying to get my bearings in the sleeting dark, I tripped over two GIs still faithfully watching their front and up to their knees in water. When informed that their company had departed some hour before they heaved themselves up out of their little sump and departed with the comment: 'Ah shit, those cocksuckers don't tell you nuthin'.

Four in the morning found me squatting beside the forward Bren gun on the summit amid the few stunted trees. Visibility was almost nil as rain-laden clouds drove across the wild sky with a moon that looked as wet as we were flickering fitfully. The odd gun fired and the occasional shell moaned for-lornly above. Flat soggy bangs came from far out in no-man's land and the trees dripped steadily. Asleep and utterly spent, sitting on a box in the gunpit, his legs in the water and mud, lay the No 2. Behind the Bren which gleamed dully whenever the moon shot through, his back propped against the dripping mud, his collar turned up uselessly, stood Fusilier Royle. Small and bespecta-cled, soaked and subdued, little Geordie Royle stood deep in the muck peering myopically into the unknown dark.

Foulmouthed cursing at weather and at fate had long since dried within me, so I only remarked with great feeling: 'Not much of a life, is it Royle?' as I sat glumly beside him. The little half-drowned, mud-sodden terrier looked at me through misted glasses. 'No sir, but I suppose someone has got to do it.' Feeling exactly three inches tall and knowing that a better man had handed me yet another lesson, I rose and squelched off to the next section.

Chapter 17

The Gesso Ridge

The first rains of the winter had fallen on the mountains and the Irish Brigade prepared to endure conditions similar to those of the Western Front in the First World War while the High Command still sought opportunities to launch an offensive.

RAIN, EVEN Italian rain, cannot last forever and the day shone clear and warm and if we had cursed that mountaineering in the dark, we now blessed the vertical crest behind which we dried out and diverted muddy streams downhill. Vertical banks meant immunity from shellfire and, generally, from mortar bombs.

Apart from manning an OP on the crest beside the artillery officers' peephole, we all dried, ate and dozed like rabbits outside the big warren. The German gunners were however inventive of mind, for as they skimmed our crest and we stood watching the *overs* bursting against BHQ in the valley, not without some pleasure expressed by Fusilier McGee with 'I hope that fucking Adjutant's shitting himself', they altered their dials and with their uncanny precision cracked airbursts over our heads.

I had long cherished an illogical contempt for airbursts and was inclined to look on them as bogeymen, all noise and no danger, but when something whacked into the mud and a shout came from the artillery OP, I revised my theory and hugged the bank with the rest. The artillery officer had caught it and the splinter had laid open his neck and shoulder like the slash of a billhook. Maurice Crehan, viewing his first battle casualty, was all solicitude, calling for dressings and stretchers, kneeling beside the wounded man. Seeing me standing there he called 'Get a drink of water for him' and without thinking I passed him my waterbottle from my belt. When this refreshment gurgled down into his guts our casualty stiffened, coughed and exuded ruddy health. Cherry brandy at least six months old is a great reviver and, as his glow of well-being spread, he offered to get up and walk down to the doctor, despite the blood all over his face and tunic.

The reserve company, D, came up one night and had a bloody little affray around a farm in front of our position, but we were left at peace until relieved some days later.

The whole front was static now while heads were scratched to find some way of getting off this last range of hills and down into the Plain of Bologna. But the Germans had once again produced their fire brigade and the dreaded words *Para Division* appeared in the intelligence reports at regular intervals.

Our next relief was of the Guards Brigade who were hanging on to a corpse-strewn crag called Monte Battaglia. But, as ever, the Escort to the Sovereign had risen above their daily dosage of dirt, cold and death, for while Maurice talked to the outgoing captain of the Welsh Guards, a large sergeant-major bustled among the trenches and dug-outs, ordering his guardsmen to tidy up empty tins and discarded broken equipment, otherwise 'what will this new lot think of us?' As one of 'this new lot' I had my own thoughts when I later saw their cemetery down by the road. There, in a democracy undreamed of by Caterham, lay the Peer and the Guardsman side by side, as they had fought and fallen: 'Into thy hands, O Lord'.

Now the head scratching had produced the answer; a John L Sullivan left and right was the way out of the impasse. The left was to be aimed at Monte Grande, a gigantic mountain crowned with a ruin, which was the province of the Blue Devils (88th) and Custer's Division (85th) while the right hook, provided by us, was to grab Monte Spaduro. Then the road would be open for one of their beloved black arrows to trundle on its wheels and gasoline into the plain, leaving us behind to make love to our mules and mountains. But down at 7 Platoon level, strung out in a single file along the Gesso ridge, such considerations made no impression at all. The Gesso ridge really educated us as to the meaning of mud and for a little while we touched hands with that generation that floundered and died around Passchendaele. Mules bogged in the filth were simply shot and left, abandoned tanks were up to their turrets and presumably eventually sank altogether; troops whose trousers and boots were clawed off their legs by its grip aroused no comment, and the doctor who had the wounded dragged back on a sledge over the slime deserved a medal.

The Argylls went ahead of us to clear a spur on Acqua Salata and in the artificial moonlight from the searchlights we waited and fretted. A whispered 'Mister Gunner, Mister Gunner wanted up front' came back from crouching figures along the track and, watching the mortarfire crashing down on Acqua Salata, I feared the worst as I stumbled and slithered up the waiting column. At the head of it I found the company runner and looked around anxiously for Maurice Crehan. The runner pointed to a figure up the bank and whispered 'he wants you' and there, face down, peering over the edge, was Sir Henry. Crawling and cursing I joined him and following his pointing finger saw below the bank the bottom half of a corpse, blown clean in two. It was stark naked and the testicles and penis were swollen to elephantine size. Sir Henry hissed in my ear: 'He must have had a good dose of pox before that shell got him' and resumed his scrutiny of the noisome object. I asked tersely and angrily if 'You sent back a message and dragged me all this way just to look at that bloody thing?' Sensing my irritation he bristled with rage and almost shouted: 'You ungrateful bastard, I thought you would be interested'. And sliding back on to the track he turned his back to me and stormed off to rejoin his waiting company.

Chapter 18

Monte Spaduro

In October 1944 an attempt was made to break the Germans' Gothic Line and it involved the Faughs attacking Monte Spaduro. That attack was repulsed at great loss and Colin Gunner was fortunate to escape with his life. After the Spaduro episode life settled in a pattern of patrolling and waiting in those cold, wet mountains.

IT TOOK the Argylls all night to clean up the spur so it was not until dawn that we got into and around our allotted farm, one in surprisingly good condition for a change. While we did so, C Company filed past to occupy a small ridge near to us. Whilst ferreting about in the cow-byre and propping Brens out of holes and windows, the CSM appeared in the doorway and called out to me: 'Your friend, Mister Doyle, has had it'. There was no noise of shelling or MG fire, all was quiet. 'What do you mean – had it?' It was all too true, however, Dick had trodden on one of those filthy Schu-mines and was minus a foot. The farm, mud and ridge faded from view and I saw the lights and colour of the Barbarini Palace with Dick swinging that pretty Irish girl around in a jig. I was thankful they had taken him back before I finished in the cowshed and came out to inspect our surroundings: better to always keep that picture of another whose friendship I had come to treasure.

If we had known what lurked in and around that quiet little shack named Spinello not very far in front we would not have been so casual that day as we inspected Spaduro and Ridge 387 across the valley. Even a Grade 3 shot could have sniped any one of us, but Spinello lay silent and inscrutable with its German garrison. By nightfall the plot had been hatched and details arranged. A Company, followed by B, were to cross the valley and storm the heights in the darkness, while C attacked Spinello behind us. Even while forming up, the mines claimed another and this time it was CSM Crowley of B Company who died in the cowshed as Father Dan murmured the last absolution. With my platoon sergeant, Shannon, I was deputed to lead the way and a strange sensation of fulfilment came to me. At long last I had come to the very edge of it all, that rim of the world where one could easily fall off. Now, at last, absolutely nothing was out there except Germans whose duty was to kill or maim me. Do not, I beg you, think that this feeling was in any way related to those figures of the comic-strip and films, anxious and eager to slay the foe. Such people may exist although I never met any. Rather it was like a child, warned again and again never to go near the ruins by night, that I stood shivering in the owl-screech under the broken postern while every fibre screamed 'Go back!' We plunged into the valley, crossed the stream and, expecting a hail of hand grenades in the face, scaled the steep approach. There was no sound save the wind in the grass and the odd shell overhead although over on the left Monte Grande blazed and thundered under the phosphorous shells as the Americans battled their way to the summit.

With Sergeant Elliott bringing his platoon up on the left and Major Crehan just behind, we moved along the ridge. Almost at once we found them and Elliott's and my Bren gunners were banging away as we overran several trenches full of Germans. The wilderness swept us along and I thought we must have caught them on the wrong foot when I fell into a trench containing four Germans, with a Spandau, facing the wrong way. Blind now to everything except that tiny universe in front of us we crashed on, collecting more prisoners and killing and wounding some who, made of finer mettle, showed fight, but it did not seem long before we stood panting and excited on the end of the ridge.

Maurice appeared and said we were where we should be, so while he installed his radio-man in a German trench and Al and Sergeant Elliott collected more prisoners, I took a guess at my bearings and strolled towards some noise in our rear, calling: 'This way C Company', only to have a rifle fired point-blank in my face. Returning to Maurice with some speed I informed him that no friends of ours lay in that direction. He waved me to shut up while he crouched over the radio, then, turning to me, said: 'They want the prisoners back at all costs. You're to take them'. To that simple and routine message I owe, perhaps, my life. Calling Lance-Corporal Cross and four of my platoon, I marshalled the little column, asked Sergeant Shannon to keep an eye on No 7, and set off. I headed the file with a young German sergeant who spoke some English, but our ripening friendship was cut short when a Spandau hit us at close range and he and two of his comrades were blown over the cliff in a hail of bullets. An hour later, down by the stream, harried all the way by a patient sniper, I knew we were really lost. Strangely enough the remaining Germans clung to my coat-tails with more confidence than Cross or the escort; but then Cross and the boys knew me.

To get any sort of a route was elementary now, and speeded up by several German shells, we set off towards the glow of the searchlights. Maps, tracks, compass, all went to the wind while we struggled towards home, any home. We had searchlights, they had not, so we set our course towards that glow in the sky and blessed the man who thought up the idea. When a shattered farm loomed up, I muttered to Cross that 'I don't care who is in there, we're going in', for the way home now seemed endless. The prisoners and escort waited outside while Cross and I pushed a door cautiously ajar. That instinct that divines a room containing humans came over me, but no sound came as we stepped inside. With roaring lungs I struck a match and Cross aimed his Tommy-gun at a pile of blankets beside which stood a pair of jackboots. I had already lost three prisoners but here obviously was one to make up the deficiency and I crashed my Luger muzzle into the heap with a force that nearly broke my wrist. With a wailing screech a small Italian shot out of the pile, took one terrified look at us and vanished out of the door. He tripped over a waiting German who, very sensibly, grabbed him and returned him to the room, kicking and screaming and quite convinced that his last moment had come. So frightened was he that despite my attempts to find out where the Gesso Ridge lay he could do nothing but invoke his saints, both general and particular, only pausing to beg the Germans for his life.

Then, as we all squatted with the unspoken comradeship of the front line in the room, and I determined to stay there for the duration if need be, a tank engine revved up far away and in the first streaks of dawn we found the ridge and got directions from a bogged tank crew. Rather cockily I led the little band down to our farmhouse, now containing the colonel and BHQ, and was surprised to be greeted by Colonel Horsfall with: 'Thank God you are alright'. While we had floundered and blundered out in no-man's land groping our way back, the counter-attack on the battalion had started and both A and B Companies were being over-run. But my little adventures were of no interest to those around the farm who were calling for artillery support and dodging the now-steadily mounting German fire. I made myself scarce at the back of the cowshed and cadged cigarettes from some mortar crews while all hell now broke loose around our farm and Spinello.

Still on the scrounge and not having had a meal for a long time I wandered hopefully back into the cowshed and sat down, just as a heavy shell hit the wall. Copying my colonel by wearing a soft cap nearly finished my career, when a beam hit the back of my head and I passed out in a cloud of dust and falling bricks. Coming to, and feeling my head, I saw that matters were indeed serious when Colonel Horsfall, picking himself up, remarked with unusual irritation 'this dust really does get in my pipe' as he cleaned out the bowl and flicked the stem. But by midday I knew that we had sustained a good hiding. C Company had to be got back under a smoke barrage and all news of my company and B had stopped.

I saw the amazing Corporal Borrett crawl back with a stomach wound then die from the effort. I almost burst out laughing at one fusilier's face as, digging away madly with a pick, he stopped petrified when he saw a Teller mine in line with his next blow. I saw a body in the OP with face covered by a gas-cape and, on asking who had bought it now, felt very saddened to be told it was Captain Chambers. Poor old Jack, one of our Canadians and a delightful man; I was hailed by him ten minutes later when he rose from his exhausted sleep and resumed duty. When the dark came at last the colonel quietly spoke to me out of the shadows: 'Take the company back Colin'. Calling Cross and the others together I set off along the ridge to Sassaleone, food and safety. Twenty-four hours before I had been part of a rifle company – A Company – of three officers and seventy men. I was taking that company home now – Lance Corporal Cross and eight men.

During the night others straggled in and, in the end, it was found that the battalion had lost 146 men. Maurice lay dead on the ridge with the others of A Company; Al and the CSM were on their way to a German cage; Dick Jefferies, the major of B Company, was a prisoner too and, still faithful to his belief that 'someone has got to do it' Fusilier Royle had died behind his Bren gun, doing it to the end.

Last of all to turn up was Sir Henry and his batman, MacNamara. Coming as he did from a long line of survivors, Sir Henry had been found by the Lancashire Fusiliers after his company had been overwhelmed. As he and MacNamara scrambled down the mountain and made tracks for home a German, stick grenade in hand, leaped out on them from some bushes. He shouted: 'Surrender, Englishmen, surrender', only to be answered by MacNamara who shot him full in the face with his Tommy-gun and replied in a phrase that deserves to live as long as Shannon flows: 'Surrender be fucked – and I'm not an Englishman'.

After the shipwreck, the salvage began to restore the battalion as a fighting unit. Two good hidings had fallen on us by now, the Trigno and now Spaduro, and it had been my luck to have survived both of them. I think it was then that that change came over me that came to all who started to count their close ones in the past, and to look at tomorrow with clouded eyes, and it was then I wrote that letter home 'to be posted in the event of my death'. But we were a regular battalion and from time to time those often-criticised, so easily and cheaply lampooned regulars had taken their hidings, picked themselves up, buried their dead and soldiered on. 'Close in on the Colours', that Ark of the Infantry's Covenant, was as real to those Old Faughs as it had been to the drunken, often flogged toughs who shuffled closer to their riddled ensigns on that bloody ridge of Albuhera while the dying Inglis screamed: 'Die hard, 57th, die hard!' Let those who see only their faults and irritating mannerisms never forget that.

We could only muster three weak companies now, and I found myself with Hogan and Sir Henry in B Company to whom came Tony Morris as major. He was viewed at once by Hogan with suspicion and by Sir Henry with outrage, since Morris had an English accent. I kept my mouth shut, did as I was told and saw that Tony Morris was a regular, a disciplinarian, and already twice decorated. Also, I sensed at once that his shoulder was not for crying on. A box of chocolates from Al's unknowing mother arrived just then, one of the regular delivery to her soldier son, now on black bread and German stew. Sir Henry promptly suggested that news of his capture be withheld from his parents so that deliveries could continue and eyed Al's expensive-looking kit hungrily, as he hoed into the chocolates. His practical suggestion was coldly ignored.

Sir Henry also shouted 'Malingerer' when I told Tony Morris that a wall suddenly went slantwise as I looked at it, causing me to fall over. The wall was quite vertical but the bash on the head from that beam had given me concussion. Still pursued with Sir Henry's comments about 'rats running away' I boarded an ambulance and went back to a Casualty Clearing Station. The CCS was only in tents pitched in mud back near Florence but I never felt so warm and safe in all my life as I lay under a blue blanket and listened to the lash of the rain on the canvas while a stove glowed and a sister asked me if I would like a cup of cocoa. I was a fraud of course, when X-rays were taken and eyes tested, but even a fraud can be grateful. It was only five days but every moment was cherished and hoarded – smoking happily and talking to a captain of the Frontier Force Rifles in the next bed. Sir Henry's faith in the army was restored when he saw me back with the company and he whooped: 'Saw through you, eh? No Base Hospital for you, you damned Sassenach – smart doctor that'. His joy was shortlived and his cackles of mirth were cut short when Hogan was sent away on leave to the UK, leaving him and me to go with Tony and the company back to the now captured Spaduro to relieve the granite northerners of the Lancashire Fusiliers.

Hogan's departure put Sir Henry in a towering rage so that when he arrived in a broken farm, on a position very close to the Germans, he relieved the waiting Lancashires by briefly telling the lieutenant in command: 'You can fuck off now, the men have come'. This not unnaturally upset this gentleman, so without further ado he called his platoon out and set off without giving the smouldering Sir Henry the benefit of his local knowledge. Fortunately the level-headed Fred Mundy, Sir Henry's long-suffering sergeant, whom he was wont to address in his cups as 'you wee whore' had words with the Lancashires' sergeant who told him on no account to move by day and only to use a hole cut in the wall at the back to go to Company HQ in the gully.

After burying his head in a blanket and having a fag, while Mundy posted the sentries, Sir Henry decided to visit Company HQ to lodge further protests with Tony. Mundy told him about the hole. Groping in the dark he located a spot where the bricks had been cut away and attempted to scramble through. His broad shoulders and equipment stopped him, so he hissed to the faithful MacNamara: 'Shove, Mac, shove'. MacNamara applied his shoulders to Sir Henry's backside, helped by Mundy, who would have preferred to apply his boot, and with this help Sir Henry popped cork-like from the hole and fell full-length and face down in a pit that had been used for two weeks by the Lancashires as a latrine. There were two holes – the escape hole and the lavatory hole; Sir Henry had backed the wrong horse.

When I scrambled through the correct hole next morning, sent by Tony to do OP duty in the farm roof, I saw Sir Henry sitting alone in a corner while even the loyal MacNamara shrank from contact with his master. My cheery 'Christ, you smell like a sewage farm' earned me a glare of stark hatred from eyes glittering madly above ordure-encrusted mustachios. We remained there a week with only rain puddles and tins of ration water to wash and cook with, while Sir Henry ripened before our eyes.

Up in the roof Sergeant De Negri sat with his glasses and telephone to the mortar line behind. I joined him on the bale of straw and idly watched the silent front. There it all was again – another Promised Land, the Plain of Bologna. How many times had we gazed from such places always thinking how easy it would be to stroll down those last slopes and motor along those straight roads for ever? Dreaming, and wondering what 'they' were doing in all those silent villas and villages spread before my eyes, I barely heard the whump of a mortar burst in front, but with every sense alert now, I heard the one that burst behind. Someone out of somewhere whispered: 'Get down, it's a bracket' and I got up from the bale and crawled over the broken beams to the ladder. Even as I lowered myself to the first rung the roof exploded and I landed at the bottom amid Sir Henry's men with a crash, as dust and splinters flew.

Silence fell, from above, with drifting dust and ominous quiet. Back up the ladder I climbed and called to De Negri, but he still sat, now smashed against the wall, dead and riddled, while the black scar of the mortar impact showed clearly on the bale of straw we had shared. Should I have shared my whisper? I wondered then, as his blanket-wrapped body went back that night on a mule, and I wonder now.

Patrols, the curse and cross of the infantry, were ordered and we were told to go and look at the 'Twin Tits', a pair of hillocks out in front of us. When summoned to Tony's dugout to organise this midnight mischief, Sir Henry flourished his famous patrol book. All his expeditions out into no-man's land were carefully recorded and exaggerated, to ensure that he was not sent out when it was not his turn. By addition, logarithms and differential calculus he triumphantly proved to an amazed Tony that it was my turn to do the patrol. Tony pointed to me sitting on an ammo box, coughing my lungs up and snivelling with a cold, and curtly remarked above my deafening barks: 'Every German for five miles can hear him coming'. 'Pah, too many cigarettes, nothing wrong with him, and anyway it's not my turn' and, rising, Sir Henry stumped away.

I was taken aback at Tony allowing this to pass so easily but was flabbergasted when he said: 'Let him go, I'll do it for you'. Majors don't do patrols except big ones; it was a lieutenant's, or sometimes a sergeant's, job, but leaving me snuffling and hacking in his dugout he went off into the night and returned at dawn covered with mud from head to foot. While waiting I wondered what would happen if the colonel turned up and found me sitting there, as I was sure that Tony had not told him he was going out. So I was relieved to see his soaking figure slide down the bank and light up his beloved pipe. Sir Henry's only comment was: 'More fool him, he should have sent you, you lead-swinging sod', as he twirled his smelly whiskers.

But even that bible of patrols did not save him when, after a few days back in the castle of Castel del Rio, we found ourselves up on Monte Grande where patrolling and raids began in earnest and those old friends from the German parachute division gave us a few lessons in the art. While in the castle Sir Henry met a worthy adversary, a major of the Skins who alleged to know him from his origins in County Cork. The major brought down the house when he flatly stated that Sir Henry had been sacked from his job in an Irish bank for dangling a fishing rod out the back window and sipping Bushmills while angry farmers beat on the locked doors with their blackthorns. Sir Henry's protests were drowned in roars of laughter, but there were some moments when the wigs nearly went on the green, as he and the Skins' major continued wordy warfare over the punch. The last and decisive shot came from the Skin. Departing he surveyed the bristling Sir Henry and remarked: 'You are typical of a lot of 'em – steal the cross from the shoulders of Christ to fire a whiskey still'. I only add that this major stood six feet two inches tall and was built in proportion. But the shadows were closing on this rich lode of gold and green that had cheered me and infuriated others during those dark, damp and dangerous weeks.

Sent to hold a position which was kept under a constant smoke cloud, he collapsed with bronchial pneumonia and, untypically, departed on a stretcher, gasping for air and for the first time wordless. But his accents rang for a long time among us and even now ring enriched down the tunnel of the years. One day, freed forever from this mortal coil, he will carouse with Emmet and the Big Fellow and in their mirth will rise the deathless song that no gallows, no famine, no exile, no dangers will ever silence.

I hope they let me eavesdrop.

Chapter 19

The Last Winter

Life in the Italian mountains in the final winter of the war was miserable and dangerous. The danger was heightened by the regular patrols into no-man's land, some of which were led by Colin Gunner. Christmas was a brief interlude of peace as Irish pipes and German hymns rang out over the snow-covered mountains.

THE DUKE of York would have recognised us during those long weeks when we marched up and down the mountain, into the line on tour of duty and out to rest billets. We were always in and out of the same sector, so much so that we could get quite cross to find a carefully domesticated trench or dugout neglected by other owners in our absence. Generally B Company had the left hand sector where the Black Ridge shot out of the battalion positions and joined up with the German para positions at the other end. It was our 'Bridge of Sighs' for those who, nightly, lay out in the snow and freezing slush, numbed and shivering and hoping that the Germans were staying in their warm billets that night.

Subject to all those fears and grotesque imaginings that patrols suffer from, I did my share of these excursions and like all the rest lay rigid, biting my hand and totally convinced beyond all doubt that waiting Germans were watching us. There were good patrol leaders, Unwin of the Faughs, Fay and Montgomerie of the Rifles, to name three but I was not one of them, although I never pulled the old trick of getting out of sight and holing up for the night before coming back with a pack of lies. But I hated it; I hated the cold and the dark; above all I hated the loneliness. The men hated it too, as they knew too well that anyone hurt during these visits to no-man's land was nearly always left behind in the fracas to die or, if lucky, to be picked up later. To myself I admitted also that whereas an attack was infinitely more dangerous, there was a feeling of all being together and of someone, in our case the major, giving orders: too much imagination or the mentality of a born follower I suppose. The use of patrols will be argued as long as they are sent out but they call for a peculiar brand of courage which I for one did not have.

B Company possessed two smashed buildings in the area and we drew the Casa di Sopra which we shared with some dead infantry of the 1st Division and four dead bullocks. The infantry we buried on the back of the slope with the usual rough cross and pencilled names, but the bullocks were another matter. Too big to drag away or bury they lay in the smashed ruin, their balloon bellies burst and rigid legs stuck up in the air. We just got used to them and the cold kept down the smell.

Night and morning with a slide-rule accuracy a German Spandau hammered our dwelling with a fixed line; so accurately that McEvoy told me that he intended to lie behind the bullocks with one finger showing above. Then, having sustained an honourable nick, he would report himself as a battle casualty. I told him to do it by all means, but added that a dead bullock seemed a pretty shaky rampart from the stream of lead arriving at twenty rounds per second. He saw the logic and lay flat behind the ruins with the rest of us.

Then one night Tony Morris went out on the Black Ridge and fell over a cliff, smashing a knee. As the only remaining officer, that promoted me to company commander. Despite the nightly issue of rum, spirits were pretty low and one night, after some heavy shells had just missed our ruin, I found myself leaning against the wall gazing across the wasteland and up at the icy stars murmuring: 'Oh Christ, get me out of this, just for a week, but please get me out of it. Oh Christ, give me pneumonia'.

With the eternal miracle of the dawn and some rum-spiked tea it all passed, and of course I was the healthiest man in the battalion. The next night we were relieved by the Rifles, and I handed over to Ted Griffiths, a Rifles' major after the company had gone back under the sergeant-major. It was a most unsatisfactory hand-over too, when the 'phone exploded in my ear and a furious adjutant asked why in the name of hell I had not given Griffiths the artillery defensive fire zones from my map. It was no good saying that Tony Morris, departing in pain, had merely shoved the map in my hand as he clutched his battered knee. I just said: 'Yes sir, sorry sir, I'll do it now at once, I haven't gone yet, sir' to which he replied: 'Well see you do, not fit to be trusted with the fire picquet'; slam! Ted smiled at my scarlet face and grunted 'Sounds his usual self', took the map and settled his company in.

Snow, Germans, mud, shells, now that bloody Prussian all boiled in my brain as I slid down the mountain to the mule-point. There was also, subconsciously, the knowledge that he was dead right and self-contempt for that pneumonia-begging moment. The nightly fixed Spandau blurted out when I was near the bend in the track and a shower of the overs spattered all around me and whopped in the snow and mud. In a panic I jumped clear of the track and rolled to the right, straight into a seemingly bottomless bomb crater full of brown porridge. Never since that day at school when a big tough nearly drowned me in the baths have I feared water, but this slime and glue was another matter; no chance at all to get to the side, no chance to do anything but flounder and try to get some foothold. It was a deep crater and I knew I was going to drown in that stinking hole. I was going to die right there, alone in a crater on an Italian mountain. That past life before the eyes bit is a lot of rubbish; all before my mud-splashed face that mattered were those scrubby bushes up on that crater rim. They might as well have been in Outer Mongolia.

No sound I shall ever hear will sound as wonderful as the clink of metal up on the track that led to 1st Division, towards which I let out a spluttering shout. Two Jocks of the Argylls were hurrying along it towards the positions on our left and, while one held his mate's belt, the other stuck his rifle out to me and I grabbed the muzzle; a heave like a bulldozer and I sat in the scrub clutching a root in a grip like a python. One gave me a rag to wipe my face while the other gave me a cigarette, then, still only figures in the dark, they departed 'for we're late and must catch up with the company'. I never knew their names, only their regiment. Perhaps they died up on Monte Grande, or later, perhaps they are alive today somewhere; whether they live in prosperous happiness or within the walls of Barlinnie, they will never die in my gratitude.

It was some ten minutes before I set off again and skirted the slope, resigned to finding some corner at the mule-point where I could dry out and perhaps get some rum from the Rifles and then just go to sleep. The fog had come up now and trailed along the rocks and scrub, the stars were shut out, only gleams lit the way from the snow and mud puddles and the guns were muttering benediction. Out of the dark and mist a voice spoke sharply: 'Is that you, Colin?' and going closer to the voice I saw a familiar silhouette, a silhouette that meant more than any rum or warm corner to hide in. Peaked cap with glittering badge, fur-collared flying jacket, stick in hand, waited Colonel Horsfall. Beside him on a rock squatted his runner. With a glance at my figure he only remarked: 'Come on, we are a bit late' and turned down the slope. I followed with his runner.

Going down I blurted out that I had been going to the mule-point to see the Rifles and catch up with the battalion later, as I thought everybody would be gone. As I babbled out the last bit I could have bitten off my tongue when he looked at me and asked: 'Did you think I would leave the line with one of my officers still there?' In silence we went on and found his jeep waiting by the mules. In bitter cold that started to solidify my mud coating we went back, while he passed a silver pocket-flask to the runner and me before taking a swig himself. When we stopped by the roadside at the Brigade HQ schoolhouse he climbed out and started to go in; I waited, by the jeep, with the runner and driver. Turning round he called 'Come on' and led the way upstairs.

Pushing open a door he entered a well-lit room full of the Brigade staff from the Brigadier downwards. I followed very cautiously, leaving a trail of mud puddles on their clean floor. Greeted by the Brigadier, who looked at me with some wonder, the Colonel remarked: 'I thought you ought to see what my officers have to put up with in the line'. The Brigadier's reply was : 'Oh, yes. Give him a drink, he looks quite cold' and taking the Colonel to an inner office left me to be told by the elegant O'Rourke of the Rifles: 'Don't come near me, you dirty bugger' as he passed me a tumbler of rum.

Worse was to come when they emerged from the inner room and the Brigadier said it was time for dinner. Quite happy to be left with my now second tumbler of rum, I stood aside before being asked by the Colonel: 'Don't you want any food?' I followed the rest to a table with snowy cloth where I ate and drank all that was going under the amused eyes of the Brigadier and the baleful stares of the Mess orderlies who would have to clean up my mess. What a contrast I thought – one moment up to the neck in that deadly slush, the next having my glass filled from a decanter of wine, but I wondered how those two Jocks were faring up on Monte Grande: the night would be very long and very cold and no-one would be asking them if they would like another go at the pudding.

We were back on Grande with Norman Plymen, a tough South African farmer as company commander, when the battalion raid on a nest of hard-case German paratroops was put in. As always with the paratroops, the reaction was swift and deadly and it cost us several men. Two officers, Bert Parish, a happy Brummie soul, and Gert Coetzee, a South African, were killed, and Colonel Horsfall was wounded by mortar fire. Our company was not called on during the night so we merely sat on our ridge and watched the flashes.

From Grande too I went to get the billets ready for B Company in San Martino, a village well out of the line, and I was sorry I missed that Christmas Eve and Day when no shot fell and, dead on midnight, the German Spandaus fired tracers into the sky while bells rang out in the battered little village in their lines. When Brian Clark sent the piper to play on Christmas Day in the snowfields on the ridge the German paratroopers applauded and I wish I could have shaken hands with that Tiny Tim of the German army who wandered into our lines with a bottle of Cognac to drink a Christmas toast with his brothers of the front.

Now commanded by Murphy Palmer, an Irish squire from County Kilkenny, we had our Christmas on December 29th, 1944, and it was Murphy, accompanied by his adjutant, who made the rounds from company to company to accept a mug of rum punch at each, and down it amid a hail of cheers for him and boos and insults for the Adjutant. Serving out the turkey to the company I joined wholeheartedly in the catcalls and shouts of 'Fuck off, Nobby' which greeted him. He seemed well insulated from insult however, as he was on his third mug of poison and beamed an amiable 'Happy Christmas' to the crescendo of ill-will.

A few more tours up on Grande ended our spell on that sector; routine tours as the front had frozen solid all across Italy. Kesselring, 'Smiling Albert', the German CinC had once more bought time for his Fuehrer. While standing behind the bank one sunny, hopeful morning talking to John Beamish of C Company, a loud crash and fountain shot frozen clods high in the air and I crouched by a tree. John (Wellington and Sandhurst) surveyed the soaring lumps and ordered a nearby fusilier to 'catch'. Working on the American supply road a weary Basuto of a road-making detail looked up to see an equally coal-black face studying him from the cab of a gigantic American truck: Alabama stared at Africa and cheerily cracked: 'Hiyuh savage, where's yuh spear?'

Despite being 'not fit to be trusted with the fire picquet' I found myself once again acting as company commander, while Norman was away ill. With only Sergeant Jerry Marnell as acting sergeant-major I looked with him over the familiar route to the Clemente ford and up the mountain we knew so well. While we did so and I told him to issue rum punch that night, Colonel Horsfall and that great provider of all, Captain (Quartermaster) Maginess, came along the snowpath.

The Colonel was back from hospital; he was back in charge again. Nothing mattered now as I looked frantically around for my belt and cap but in a few words, 'I have just come to say goodbye to the company', he flattened my momentary joy. He was going to the staff at Army HQ and I stood, blank and bewildered, while he thanked the company for all that they had done for him. I sought the Quartermaster's eyes for some explanation but that lean old soldier, who saw all and knew all, only stared me down impassively. I mumbled, saluted and watched the Colonel's figure recede across the snowfields. I was utterly downcast for I knew that only once in a lifetime would I meet a man whom none could serve without being better for it.

I regretted the generosity with the rum when we set off on our last relief that night. Corporal Keenan, a platoon commander, all of nineteen years of age from Lurgan, had used his dizzy promotion to get a share in accordance with his rank. By the time we neared the Clemente ford he had worked his way through every pub ballad that ever shook the rafters of Mooney's Irish

House and the ghost of John McCormack was walking beside him. He was taking Kathleen home yet again while I waited on the far bank and the company waded across. A wild screech and splash told me that he had taken Kathleen straight into one of the few potholes of the ford.

Chapter 20

Close Quarters

> The spring of 1945 was spent along the banks of the River Senio, at times only yards from the German positions. Colin Gunner was sent as a Defending Officer to a Court-Martial Centre and then to the Divisional Battle School. He returned to the Faughs in time for the final assault in Italy as the Irish Brigade broke through the German defences to the River Po.

BAEDEKER MAY not rate Florence at the head of his Italian cities, but it was a wonderful place to us, stationed at Bivigliano some forty miles away. Here life was very placid after the months of mountains and we now had enough men to reform the old A Company again. I was not moved back into A but was quite happy where I was in B even if I would never again have my lucky 7 Platoon; now I had No 11.

Everyone got his share of visits and leave to Florence and most wandered across the Ponte Vecchio in search of Beatrice and the risk of a dose. Walking across the big square one morning it dawned on me just why it seemed such a lovely place – it was untouched. There were no bomb or shell marks anywhere. Such scars were so normal to our eyes that it came as a shock to look at the shops and arcades with intact roofs and unshattered glass; it just didn't seem right.

I perhaps saw more of the city than others as I was detailed to go as Defending Officer to the Court Martial Centre where our deserters were being tried. The maxim that the worst criminal is entitled to the best defence does not apply in the army or one of our soldier/lawyers would have got the job. This was obvious to the Court Martial President, a colonel in the Welsh Guards, who took one look at the shamrock on my arm and, taking me to one side, enquired: 'Have you done this before?' To my positive and cheerful 'No sir, detailed by the Adjutant', he smiled and remarked: 'Well, just listen to me and look up the bit about Plea of Mitigation'. I suppose it made things easier for the Court to deal with Defending Officers who only knew how to say 'Seven Days' in a company office.

In common with all the front line soldiers, deserter hatred had rubbed off on me. How could it be otherwise when, again and again, we saw good men going on, getting wounded, coming back, and using the last dregs of their courage to go on again, all too often to the end? Why was it always them, we thought as we tried to find them jobs in a little safety back at B Echelon, and watched the hand of one we knew and loved trembling as he lit a cigarette. I firmly believe that, to some, death really came as a friend 'as if almost glad the end had come'. Two contrasts come to mind of two men who were both in my platoon; one, a sergeant, wished upon me against my protests, loud-mouthed and superficially efficient when out of the line, who lasted only two tours in a quiet sector before running away. The other comes from a notebook open in front of me as I write:

> Fusilier McGee. Born 21.8.21. Embarked 22.11.42. Single.
> 3 times wounded. Serving in B Company.

I ran out of ideas for my 'Plea of Mitigation' about the second day, while the conveyor belt of cases rattled on and I sat irritably doodling and wondering when we would get a break for a cigarette while Colonel Quennell ladled out the sentences. I did take an interest however in one case. Visiting the jail that morning I was escorted down grey corridors by a staff sergeant then locked in a cell with another customer. This one I knew and knew well. He was the youngest soldier in B Company, a fair-haired, nervous boy who should have been pedalling a bike around the streets of Belfast with a meat basket on the handlebars, not sitting frightened to death, on the verge of tears, in this macaroni Dartmoor.

He really believed in the 'Prisoner's Friend', the poor, trusting little idiot. He had been hurt in the foot up on Grande and sent to the dressing station. When he came out he turned the wrong way and was picked up in the rear, heading towards Rome. To the Court's surprise, I pleaded 'not guilty' next morning and, helped by the colonel, made out that the shock of the injury had upset him and that he really meant to rejoin the company; he had just got on a truck going the wrong way. Mentally swishing my gown and adjusting a full-bottomed wig, I sat down. Colonel Quennell stared at me thoughtfully for a long moment, then turned to the prisoner: 'You have heard what one of your own officers has said. Are you prepared to go back with him now to your Regiment?' The hatless one, not quite believing it all, murmured 'Yes, sir' and left the Court with B Company's copy of Patrick Hastings. His was the only acquittal I got in ten days.

Returning to Bivigliano, I found the battalion packing up to go back into the fold of Eighth Army on the Adriatic sector so, evicting my batman Siever from the best seat, I got aboard the company jeep and, sitting behind Major Jack Phelan, rode comfortably across Italy again to the Forli barracks. Tony Morris, now second-in-command of the battalion, took one look at these peacetime barracks, tore down the Italian signboard, requisitioned every pot of paint in the division and in no time created a little Aldershot within sound of the guns up on the Senio river. It was renamed *St Patrick's Barracks* of course and only shortage of paint stopped him having the barbed-wire in regimental colours.

As for Siever, watching me drill the platoon on the square one morning, he could hardly wait to comment 'Proper little RSM, ain't we?' when I got back to the Mess. Being a batman Siever dodged all parades, to the fury of the CSM, so I crisply replied: 'Yes, and you can go and get a shave for a start'. Siever and I had settled down pretty well together once he had got me used to his ways, which included wearing my shirts and smoking my cigarettes and he was always ready to act as military adviser. I could have done with him the night I was Orderly Officer and, drinking hard in the Mess, forgot all about guard mounting as the doctor belted away on a piano. Tacking and weaving I found the Guard Room, scrawled my name on the Guard Book and was assisted back to the Mess by Sergeant Barney Phillips, who had mounted the Guard. At breakfast I sat as far as possible away from the adjutant, who would not have appreciated 'for there comes a night when the best gets tight, and then turns out the Guard'.

When he sent for me later my heart stopped and 'Barney has blabbed' flashed into my mind, but he merely looked up from his table and, after the normal stare of blue-eyed loathing, said: 'You will relieve Jimmy Trousdell at the Battle School, and I shan't tell you about that cap again'. The last referred to a crumpled and cherished peaked cap which I slept in religiously and which would have rejoiced the heart of Baron von Richthofen.

If Siever's face lit up like a Verey light at the news, Jimmy Trousdell's sank like a spent rocket when I arrived at the Battle School. 'I thought it was too good to last. Better come and see the billet' was his only comment. And looking down that lovely valley, glowing in the spring sun, I could not blame him. Siever took over while I reported to the commander, Major Jimmy Clarke, and when I got back found him established as the son of the house with his bed made up in the best room and Mama pouring him some vino. The Battle School had been set up to convert sergeants and officers from anti-aircraft regiments to infantry and, with some dozen others from different regiments, I was an Instructor – not only an Instructor but a captain. Whether we were considered the dregs or cream of the fighting units I was never sure but the days lengthened, the sun shone, and Major Clarke was very tolerant about illegal visits to Florence.

The major only put his foot down once when the visits had taken such a toll that Simmons of the Buffs used to stand speechless and glazed before his class until his sergeant hissed 'Speak now' in his ear, when he would rattle off a recitation entitled *The Platoon in the Night Attack*, pick up his stick and go to bed. Still, I had tea with a Field Marshal when the Director of Infantry visited us and I actually passed him the sugar.

What those students learned I cannot say. The blind, in the hung-over sense, led the blind, but I don't think many of them ever got to the line in time to put our splendid theories into practice. If they did they were probably killed, as were two of the tutors a few weeks later.

The Faughs meanwhile had been prised loose from St Patrick's Barracks and were leading a weird life on the Senio bank. This high floodbank, or bund, was held on one side by the Germans and on the other by the Irish Brigade. To look over the top was death, so each side spent their time heaving hand grenades over at each other. As they were so close, little artillery or mortar fire could worry them but dodging the endless hours of grenades must have made up for it.

I believe that enterprising tunnellers burrowed through into other people's dugouts and I was told that, in full daylight, a German jumped on the top and shouted: 'Cheerio, Tommy, I'm off on leave' and, before anyone could pull a trigger, leapt down again. I knew for certain that Reginald Bartlett, who had my platoon, had been shot through the head and killed by a sniper as he looked over the top at dawn for the last time.

But such rumours did not disturb Siever and myself back in Happy Valley, eating Mama's spaghetti and playing in the sun with the bambinos. However, as Jimmy Trousdell had said, it was too good to last and Siever's farewell to the family would have moved a man of flint, when orders came to close the school and get back to our battalions. On the way, while I sat listening to the news from the jeep driver, he sat in the back with tears still in his eyes.

The attack had started and the Faughs were to break out of a bridgehead made by the New Zealanders. Jack Phelan was commanding B Company with a new officer whom I did not know. Arriving at the rear BHQ I was greeted by Tony Morris, second-in-command of the battalion, and told: 'You stay here with me, Jack has got an officer – no need for you to go up' which came as a very pleasant surprise. After a leisurely breakfast we both strolled out of the billet to look at the war and watch the flights of fighter-bombers wheeling and pouncing overhead. Tony said that the battalion would be attacking at about that time. As he said this a jeep bounced up to his HQ with the new officer in it. The driver handed Tony a note which he read in silence then, turning to me, he said: 'You are to go up at once – report to the Adjutant'. I looked from him to the new chap and saw a classic case of bomb-happiness before my eyes. Bomb-happiness, shell-shock, loss of nerve or what you will, it all added up to him coming out of the line and me going in.

If I was annoyed Siever, throwing the kit on the jeep, was transported with rage. Officers were not supposed to crack, according to his book, especially if they had to be replaced with 'his bloke'. His diatribe against all commissioned ranks only stopped when he shouted to me amid the swirling dust-cloud: 'Anyway, I got his cigarettes – he won't need them in hospital' and waved two tins each of fifty Players under my nose; two tins filched from the departing one's pack.

Brian wasted no time with me at BHQ where he and Colonel Murphy [Palmer] sat listening to the reports from the two assault companies already in action; just: 'Get off that jeep. Your company is in reserve – go with the runner and find Jack'. With the runner leading the way among hedges and orchards, with the guns battering steadily away behind, and with the mutinous Siever bringing up the rear, I sought my company. But before I found Jack I found my platoon, lining a ditch under Sergeant Ray Hall and there occurred something I shall carry to the grave. They gave me a cheer on a battlefield, and the memory of that, the greatest compliment any officer of the infantry can ever hope for, can never be taken away.

We had an easy day passing through the assault companies to take the last objective but, as one returning refreshed and rested, I was the obvious patrol choice for the night. The fields, well lit by blazing farms, looked flat and endless as I picked some sort of route to the lateral road out in front. I had just spent five minutes trying to wake the commander of C Company, Pat Howard, who sat head on arms over a table. I might as well have shaken a statue. But I got to the road, after investigating some dugouts and sat there all night on the junction. Returning at dawn and reporting to Colonel Palmer I then went for what I considered to be an earned sleep.

Before the mists grew black I dimly heard: 'He's the only officer I've got, you know' coming from the company commander, and another voice replying: 'Yes – and he's had a month's rest' before Siever shook me awake for a return trip out in front to go beyond the road to a place marked as the Tobacco Factory. With the iron Corporal Nansen and six more I set off again in blazing sunshine and perfect visibility. Over the cross-roads, now friendly and warm, we plodded and found six German infantrymen at the Tobacco Factory who seemed very happy to see us. Only stopping to look round for some vino we set off back, now the owners of a donkey-cart in which I thought we would drive up to BHQ in Royal Mail style. A combination of the donkey's lack of stamina and a shrewd 'This bloody road could be mined' from Nansen put us back on our feet when a great crash came as we neared the crossroads.

When we got there we found a demoralised gang of those strange creatures who appeared in such warlike postures during the last weeks, the Partisans.

Others have told the tale, and told it fluently, of the activities of all those irregular bands who proliferated in Europe in those days, some of them doubtless of great value, all of them exponents of the mouth being mightier than the sword. The praises of three of them would never be sung as I looked at dripping shreds draped on the hedges and surveyed a crater on the cross-roads; the very junction we had sat on all night and which the Germans had thoughtfully mined. After a few moments when the surviving partisans asked, and were refused, permission to shoot my prisoners we went our separate ways, I to report back to Colonel Palmer, they to clear the way for the less colourful and less imaginative Irish Brigade.

We seemed to be getting too fond of the daylight when, two days later, we formed up to attack towards a canal. But there was an early mist which, thickened up by the barrage, screened us beautifully all the way to the objective. A German corporal thought it screened him beautifully too as he waited, grenade in hand, on the canal bank, but Jack Phelan saw him first and, calling the company sniper, had him shot through the head. The German shot in the air and rolled back over the bank. I was too involved on the left at the time, having bumped into one of their outposts and having had one of my platoon shot through the face. As soon as we got on to the canal the gunfire came down, so it was dig if outside and hug the walls if near the farm, an irresistible magnet when the shells and mortars started to come down – so much so that Jack said quietly in my ear: 'don't you want to go outside?' If I had had a shred of honesty I would have said 'no' instead of going very slowly between the explosions and lying behind the pigsty for a long time.

Before night fell Brian Clark came up and told us to hand over to the Recce Regiment at dark, but hearing about the German killed by our sniper he told Jack to get the body for identification before we left. Jack left me to do the job of rushing over the bank and getting the body back and in view of what he had said to me so quietly that morning he was doing me a favour. He led the company back at nightfall while the Recce Regiment filed in to fulfil, for them, an exciting task. I waited with two of my boys until I could see the stars before making a mad rush over the top. There he was, and with a panting heave we shot the body over and down the bank before leaping after it. It came to rest by the pigsty and while Fusilier Till held open a sandbag I ripped off the shoulder straps and emptied the pockets. Standing up, I pushed his dead hand straight with my boot and remarked: 'Well, his troubles are over' to be recalled by Till, standing with his helmet in his hand, saying: 'Yes, and I suppose he was some mother's son'.

Telling the Recce officer that he could bury the German we set off to catch up with the company, each of us 'some mother's son'.

Chapter 21

The Argenta Gap

April 1945; the final days of the war in Italy as the Faughs follow the mecha-
nised Rifles through the Argenta Gap and the German collapse begins. The
German surrender is followed by celebrations among the soldiers of the Irish
Brigade.

BEYOND OUR knowledge of events the last battle had narrowed down to a place
called the Argenta Gap and our previous skirmishing seemed insignificant
when we found ourselves up in line with the Northants waiting to attack
across a huge anti-tank ditch. While the Northants did things in real style in
Argenta with fighter-bomber support as well as flamethrower tanks, we
attacked all day with two companies and our ever faithful friends of the 17th
Field Regiment, Royal Artillery. As B Company was in reserve, I saw
nothing of this last breaking of the last line after having crawled so slowly up
the Italian peninsula.

I sat in a ditch with the platoon and waited, waited until the anti-tank ditch
had been taken and B Company was ordered to attack in the dark up to yet
another canal bank ahead of us. But if the last line was broken on GHQ's map,
it was not broken on B Company's front as we advanced on both sides of the
road under fire. We got to our first bound on a burning farm after losing some
casualties by shellfire, and three dazed Germans crawled out of an outbuild-
ing. While we roped them in, the left hand Bren gunner shouted out to me
from the hayricks and I found him with his gun pointing down the entrance to
a dugout shaft. We were all carrying grenades and one was in my hand, but
some Power stopped me from rolling it down those stairs and fourteen
Germans, hands held high, trooped out into captivity and life. Sergeant Hall
was busy while I was rooting around the ricks and the front of the next farm
exploded as his PIAT bomb hit it at a range of ten yards, wiping out a German
machine-gun crew. Once again the pure oblivion of the assault took command, an oblivion that generates an ignorance of risk, an oblivion that holds
cowardice and courage on a knife-edge: the orgasm of war.

Before we reached the canal a great flash and roar hurled the leading
section flat and I thought that someone had trodden on a mine. Next day I
called the roll as we hung on in the farm which we would not quit for all the
gold of Peru, even though it burned steadily around our ears. I could account

for everyone save *one* and in spite of every check his fate remained a mystery. It stayed so until the Rifles crashed through ahead of us in their Kangaroos and we were ordered to march on again to follow up. As we left our smouldering wreck, Sergeant Hall called out: 'What's that up on the roof?' and hanging over the eaves we saw a pair of legs. Our mystery was solved. That crash as we reached the canal had been a German bazooka hitting our missing man square on the belt-buckle and blowing half of him on to the roof; the other half we never found.

All day we marched on to catch up with the Rifles who rode to war in armoured taxis. They rode so swiftly that dismounting on a captured enemy gun battery they were able to wind the telephone and have a chat with a bewildered German officer at the other end. And it was while on this march up to Santerno for the night attack that, pulling out of the column to count heads, the feeling came to me that came to all at some time along those dusty, muddy, snowy roads and tracks. Standing aside for a few moments before being rebuked by Jack for not being at the head of the platoon, a great wave of love for those bowed, laden, dusty, slouching figures swept over me. There they were, even the one you knew would run away at the first opportunity. They couldn't drive a truck, they couldn't see their war from a tank periscope or a workshop window, their education wouldn't help them into a job at Base: they sought safety, God help them, but they were here at war's extremity where only God could stand; the crest of foam on the breaking wave. Such a thin crest for such a giant wave. But if the assault was the orgasm of war, the tired, joking, grumbling file of the rifle company was the love that endured for ever for it was sired by death and fear and common laughter. They asked for so little.

Santerno was easy. Two companies went in by night, then B and D by day to open out but not before a 105 blew Jack Phelan and me across a farmyard, Jack with a splinter under his eye and myself with a small one across the throat. It was all folding up now, but wisely this knowledge was not allowed to come down to our level. With such knowledge who could be blamed for simply sitting down and refusing to move? But even so the prayer rising day and night was 'Please God, not now? Not just at the end – please God'. I was among that chorus that rolled around the Gate of Heaven and more so when the Skins took a village by night and Norman Plymen, sent up to replace Jack as company commander, told me we were to attack next morning up to the River Po. With Norman I went to get a look at the way ahead from the bell tower, but rising out of the ladderway at the top, I heard the bell ring beside me. It was not Norman playing about with the rope but a clear bullet splash on the bell that sent us both down to view the ground from a lower and safer level.

The tanks allotted to us for the attack had a better knowledge of affairs than us so, after a show of track-rattling and turret-swivelling, they stayed behind in the orchards while we set off across the cornfields. They stayed there all day and may be there now for all I know. German tanks had also stayed but for different motives. When on the first bound we took a farm, we also took four prisoners. Roughly searching them in the kitchen I pulled out a packet of German oak leaf cigarettes from a corporal's pocket. With a sneering 'shit' I flung the packet into a rain puddle and looked at his eyes as he watched his only smoke on the way to the cage ground into pulp. Then, with 'smoke from the Englander', I gave him a tin of fifty Players: *Vae Victis.*

Corporal Nansen called me on the right and, joining him by the Bren gun, I saw a German tank over the canal bridge, his gun in line with our farm. With another confident prediction from myself, 'It's alright, it's knocked out', and another shrewd remark from Nansen, 'I've heard that before', I took four of the platoon over the bridge to claim our trophy. Not until I saw grey figures leaping into the turret did I believe it, but when he opened up with his machine-gun it became all too clear. The only thing that saved us was that we were so close that he could not depress his gun enough to kill us. That, plus the depth of the ditch, which enabled us to crawl back to the bridge. The Germans put the bridge out of bounds by blowing the coping stones out with an HE shell, so it was into the canal and swim for all save one who had never learnt that skill.

Pursued along the far bank by the machine-gun and covered with duck weed we retreated to Norman and Company HQ. While I searched for a rope the quicker-witted Fusilier Salmon had hauled our non-swimmer across with linked machine gun belts. He was rightly decorated for this and for reviving him who came across via the canal bottom.

Next morning we crossed and took the now burning tank and farm and while we searched the hayricks and buildings, and Norman and I stood by the back door I saw Death's fist crash down for the last time. The farm owner, hidden in some dugout, came out with gesticulations and applause to greet his liberators. As he babbled his joyous thanks a single rifle bullet hit him full in the chest and he went to his account on his own doorstep.

From the kalefields ahead, like a jack-in-the-box, shot a German. Running towards us he waved one of those pamphlets which guaranteed a prisoner long life and happiness by courtesy of the Allies. Passing Siever, he was greeted with: 'What are you selling, mate – the Mirror or Mail?'

Then there was a last patrol into the kale, a few shots which hit the trees beside us, and next morning John Beamish, coloured cap on his blond thatch, led C Company into Ruina on the Po banks. No shot fell when we looked at the roaring brown flood down the bank; no shot when the six-pounders were wheeled up to smash a church steeple opposite; no shot when, after a lunch of cognac, I fell asleep on my blanket by a broken wall in B Company HQ.

I awoke when the door crashed open and I saw the CSM festooned with rifles. He flung them in a corner with the remark: 'It's all over. Get their rifles off them or they'll kill themselves'. I rose, wiped my face, and poured two mugs of cognac. We shook hands and drank them down. He went out to disarm the company and I sat down alone at the table. From outside the noises had started; noises that were to crescendo into a Donnybrook of twenty miles of the Po flickering under Verey lights and mortar flares. I finished the cognac and went out to join them; to ring the bell of the church and to ride a horse into Battalion HQ; to try to let it sink in and understand that tomorrow held no barrage, no start line, no Spandaus, no death.

Suddenly in the middle of it all I knew I had to find Johnny Bowley. We had started together; I knew he was alive; I knew roughly where he was. Seizing a motorbike from a signals sergeant, who would have given me his wife, I set off. I skidded on many a track, I was pulled out of the ditch once, but the bike did not falter and I would have ridden through the Gates of Hell. I recognised a sign and with a last spurt up a farmyard there, as if expecting the occasion, he stood – on top of a dunghill, a bottle of cognac in his hand, eyes gleaming, hair tousled, cocky, indomitable, surviving Johnny Bowley. In the straw and urine I joined him and, wordless, we shook hands; wordless until Johnny lowered the bottle from his lips: 'You know skipper, sometimes I thought we wouldn't make it'.

We made it. With all our losses, we made it; losses that we can never recall. And not just the losses of those who had been beside us on the road and are beside us even now; we left behind on that road our illusions, perhaps our hopes, certainly our youth. They had to go sometime. Could we have left them in better company or safer hands?

Chapter 22

Into Austria

May 1945. The last march of the Irish Brigade takes them into the Austrian province of Carinthia and the turmoil of a country filled with enemy soldiery, refugees from the war in eastern Europe, Italy and the Balkans.

AFTER THE elation of the war's end, the parties and the booze, the battalion was to be found in dismal billets at the foothills of the Alps. My company was in a railway station and as a farewell gesture to us it rained as only Italian skies can. Standing damp and grumpy outside Company HQ one day I was hailed by Major Tony Morris, the second-in-command, from a large, looted American car. Tony had been my company commander in B Company before his elevation and he had not forgotten his old, and often only, officer in those icy nights on Monte Grande. Obeying his 'Jump in' he whisked me away to a splendid castle in the hills for tea, vino and cream cakes with a delightful family including several staggeringly beautiful girls. Tony spoke Italian and I got the impression that he was somehow related to them, but there was always a mysterious side to Tony from which no veil was lifted, at least not to me. Sitting in his dugout on a dreary hillside once he had cheered himself up by informing me that 'the trouble with you is that you never went to a decent school'. However he stood me this treat and I made a good hole in the excellent cognac.

A friend in a neighbouring battalion was approached by the locals who informed him that they were about to shoot the town secretary, a Fascist, and would he lend them some rifles to do the job? This he did, but took the precaution of attending the ceremony to ensure the return of his muskets. He was a hardened character and no lover of things Italian; his only comment was 'most interesting'.

At last we departed in glorious sunshine on troop transport lorries loaned by 6th Armoured Division. Many of the company had, as spoils of war, automatic pistols. I myself had six but I had always warned my platoon not to play at cowboys with them. Alas, en route, a short crack announced that Corporal Nansen had shot the man opposite him in the leg with his cherished Luger. The injured one was packed off with a flesh wound and I confiscated the Luger. It was unthinkable to punish Nansen as he was one of those iron NCOs who had made all our victories possible, so next day I restored his trophy to him and begged him not to shoot anyone else.

On arrival in Austria the RSM, that summit of discipline and authority, spotted a fusilier playing with one of the despised Italian Biretta automatics. With a curt 'give that to me' he took it from the owner. Safe in regimental hands he must have pressed the wrong button as there was a loud bang and a piper fell shot in the foot. The incident, like many others, was wrapped in secrecy never to be spoken of until rum and hilarity loosened tongues. I often wondered if the wounded piper was logged as a battle casualty. Only the RSM's dreaded master, the Adjutant, could answer that and no-one would risk asking *him*. On the road we passed endless columns of trudging German troops from the defeated hosts but they were tidy, respectful and disciplined. They certainly did not impede the last march of the old Irish Brigade.

The regimental motto of the Faughs, Faugh a Ballagh (clear the way) seemed very apt just then but what a small handful in the battalions had come from start to finish. In the Royal Irish Fusiliers it was less than fifty of all ranks.

From drummer to general the contrast on entering the beautiful country of Austria was not unremarked. As we crossed the frontier the difference was before our eyes in one mile – just one mile. Where we had seen only mud and squalor, cleanliness now held sway. Where shattered barns and tank-blasted farms had been to us the norm there now lay red-tiled roofs, clean paintwork and gardens. Green fields, neat hayricks and soaring white mountains beckoned and, for a moment, I saw the Gesso ridge with its sea of filth, foundered mules and mud-sodden wounded. Poor old Italy, you paid the price for your dagger-thrust at stricken France and reeling Britain, but above all poor old *contadini* peasants in those barraged hovels we knew so well. We *did* feel for you as we slaughtered your last chicken and gave your scrofulous brats an army biscuit. You were no '*hyena frisking at the heels of the Teutonic legions*'. You only asked for a mess of spaghetti and a flask of vile-tasting vino. Just thank God for your unforgettable and unconquerable *Mamas* who knelt before lurid statues of Our Lady with the rosary between their toil-twisted fingers.

At the head of the Regiment rode Brian Clark, the Adjutant and Tony Morris, the second-in-command the CO having gone ahead. Flying from their jeep was a guidon in regimental colours embossed with the eagle and if the War Office had possessed a shred of imagination *that* would have been the Colours. The troops were like convent children on a day's outing and, looking at their scrubbed faces, clean khaki-drill, white belts and polished brasses, it was permissible to feel proud that they obeyed and looked to their officers. Dear God, I was all of twenty-two!

As the battalion halted in some dream village buried in an endless sea of apple blossom, a splendid figure rode up on a motorbike. He was a *Sturmbannfuehrer*, or major, of the *Waffen SS* and among his decorations was the *Ritterkreuz*, the German VC. He told Brian Clark that he wished to surrender his battalion and, as my company had not debussed, we were ordered to go with him to investigate. We had no maps, so Jack Phelan, Fred Lafferty, another lieutenant, and myself put our trust in God and the SS officer and set off eastwards. At a road fork some miles on the major halted and indicated that we go with him on foot across a farm. He also indicated that down the right fork were the Cossacks near the village of Lavamuend.

Jack sent Lafferty with his platoon into the embrace of the riders of the steppes and, with me and my platoon, set off across the fields with our formidable guide. In the farmhouse was a company of Turcoman SS (NATO was not invented by the Allies) who were drunk to a man but von Reiss, for that was the SS major's name, brushed them aside although not before I secured a red fez embroidered with the death's head. I also had a swig from a proferred bottle of vile *arrak*. Any doubts we may have entertained about von Reiss's veracity were dispelled as we turned at the curve of a railway line; he indeed had a battalion. He also had an armoured train, a battery of field-guns and five Panther tanks which his men were unloading from the flat-cars – not only unloading but passing the cannon shells into the turrets. Von Reiss had a small army.

Let me digress for a moment. To those who did not know, all SS were not concentration camp guards, heaving babies into gas-chambers or thugs in leather coats bashing David Niven with rubber truncheons. Those were the *Allgemeine SS* and any lout could join them. We were meeting *Waffen* – or fighting – *SS*, the crack combat troops of the Third Reich. Well-equipped and superbly disciplined they had, apart from the Parachute Divisions, no equal in the regiments of the brave German army: ask any who fought them in the Bocage and Caen for confirmation. When all was lost they fought on for Fuehrer and Fatherland and if that be a crime I would like to think that the Brigade of Guards would have perished around the King in the ruins of Buckingham Palace if the United Kingdom had gone down in ruins.

Von Reiss explained that as Lavamuend was infested with 'Bulgar scum' he proposed to attack it and clear them off Austrian soil. 'It would only take an hour', then he would surrender to us. Looking at his men and equipment I privately thought that it would take him ten minutes, and I mean no disrespect to my own distinguished regiment when I say that that battalion of *Reichsfuehrer Waffen SS* was the most formidable unit I saw at any time I wore the King's coat. They had passed from being soldiers into fighting machines. Jack, overawed by the show of might and backed only by Lieutenant C C Gunner and twenty-five fusiliers rose nobly to the occasion and dissuaded von Reiss from his projected bloodbath despite my muttered 'For

Christ's sake be careful, these buggers are their own law'. Jack was always a bull at a gate but some hundreds of Bulgars can thank that brave and burly South African for their lives.

Later, when I saw the Bulgars at close quarters, I was sorry that the SS did not slaughter the lot. Von Reiss then asked Jack for permission to parade his men for the last time and his battalion formed up in a hollow square. As they did so my runner came up and said that a German officer wished to speak to me. I told him to bring him to where I stood with Jack and von Reiss. He returned to say that the German was on parade and 'could not break ranks'. *Ho, Ho,* thinks I, here is that spirit of old Prussia of which I had read as a boy, so I went where Fusilier Siever indicated. The German crashed to attention and saluted. He then said that his father, a colonel, had laid down his pistol to the Russians and been immediately shot. He wished to retain his pistol as he understood that was allowed under the terms of surrender. I looked at his shoulder-straps and then pointed out that he was not an officer but a *Fahnrich* or officer cadet and should therefore lay down his pistol. I also asked if he thought I was a 'bloody Russian?' This last horrified him and he stammered: 'Nein, nein, lieibe Gott, nein' as he laid his Luger down.

Von Reiss then addressed his soldiers for the last time and although I speak no German I sensed it was not as a crushed, demoralised mob that they parted but as men who had done their duty to the end. He then passed down the ranks and shook hands with every man; many were in tears and several broke down openly. Then he called them to attention, turned and saluted Jack and said that they were ready to march off. Jack told him that he could travel back with him in the jeep which had been sent up to us. His reply was magnificent: 'I have marched with these men for four years. I march with them now.'

Before they went I hastily asked that his only two officers be left with me, as I had thought of other units that might be in the area and who might not obey me but would listen to their own superiors. This was agreed and the two *Obersturmfuehrers* – lieutenants – stayed behind. Jack departed in the jeep with the all-embracing order to 'keep an eye on this place' while the SS column swung off singing their battle chants. As their voices died away I thought of the epitaph of Napoleon's Old Guard – *Defeated they may be; broken never.*

The warriors were now smiling happily. The major had departed and so we could get down to the real business – looting. The train had also carried some two hundred refugee farmers from the Balkans who were told to clear off with hand baggage only; their other possessions in the coaches now awaited the attention of No 11 Platoon, B Company. I asked the two SS officers to step into the coach which I grandly designated as Platoon Headquarters and to take their ease. Siever was told to stay and entertain them with Players cigarettes, tea and rum. The ritual brew-up had gone on throughout the surrender ceremony and I know that if the Irish Brigade had ever marched past The King there would have been some blackened brew-cans bubbling behind HM with a smiling Bud Maginess, the Quartermaster, pouring a tot of rum into each. So it was now, as we got down to business.

The heap of surrendered Lugers and field-glasses vanished after their good lieutenant and his sergeant had had first cut, then the train was ransacked. Fusilier McGee opened a suitcase and pulled out a complete Leica camera set, telescopic lenses and all. He smiled broadly when I offered him £10 for the lot and put it under his arm. McGee would have been puzzled by a five shillings Box Brownie but rank hath no privileges when it comes to the spoils of war. Wellington knew that at Vittoria when a soldier of the Faughs seized the baton of a Marshal of France and only the threat of flogging recovered it for the King of England.

It was a happy hour and rooting about in that glorious Austrian sunshine was some little bonus for the bitter drenching days of the previous winter. I did not come out of it very well but I did secure the SS Standard which now hangs in the regimental museum. The best came last as one cattle truck was found to be secured with padlocks. That was no problem to even the newest joined fusilier and I led the way into Ali Baba's cave where case upon case of French champagne and brandy stood before us, all stamped *Reservée pour le Wehrmacht*, as well as a large crate of eggs and, rather mysteriously, a cooked side of lamb and leg of pork and a tub of excellent butter. *Sod the rations*, we thought, even if they did remember to send us any, which they didn't!

After a large meal of cold meat and eggs fried in butter the champagne was broached and it would have broken a great somelier's heart to see it sloshed into tin mugs and drunk with comments such as 'same as fucking pop, ain't it'; 'chuck some of that brandy in Paddy – it livens it up'. Dusk was falling now and, after posting two unsteady sentries to patrol the train, I remembered my guests. They sat quietly in the carriage still wearing their pistol-belts but when Siever produced supper and laid places for the three of us they brightened up; Siever even produced a jar of pickles from God knows where and a loaf of black bread. I placed three bottles of champagne and three of brandy on the table and apologised for the tin mugs. They both knew where it all came from but they took off their belts, hung them within reach and an officer of HM King George and two of Chancellor Hitler fell to. If I was damn hungry, having gone all day on cigarettes and tea, they were more so and made a good dent in their/our cold lamb. The champagne was used to wash it down so I put out more.

I now studied these two prisoners more closely. The tall one spoke good

English and wore the Iron Cross, first and second class, the wound badge and another, embossed *Krim,* for the Crimean offensive. His sleeve bore the armband *Reichsfuehrer SS*; his black dress cap with the death's head badge hung by his belt but his uniform was field grey and very like our own khaki drill. His comrade was short and stocky with cropped fair hair and was younger, about twenty-two I would guess. His uniform and decorations were identical but he wore in addition the *Ritterkreuz mitt Eichenlaub*, the Knight's Cross with Oakleaves, a very high award for bravery. I could see that he understood English but would not speak it to me. We pushed away the mess-tins, loosened collars and uncorked the brandy. Thanks to my dear platoon sergeant, Jerry Hall, who did not smoke we had plenty of cigarettes which, after their oak leaf substitutes, were appreciated by the Germans. We talked at random of this and that and I observed that their capacity for the hard stuff showed that they had heads like a Krupp cannon-ball; and I was no mean judge by then of such matters. My last recollection before we all sprawled comatose on the couches was to ask of the tall one where his friend had won the *Ritterkreuz*. He answered 'In Russland, of course'. I then asked where they had seen the heaviest fighting. The *Ritterkreuz* holder spoke sharply in German and his comrade looked embarrassed. 'What did he say?' I asked. He hesitated and said: 'You have treated us like officers and honourably. I do not wish to insult you'. Well insulated from insult by then I pressed my question. 'Very well, he said that unless you were in the *sturm* [assault] on Sevastopol you have never known war'. I grandly replied that honest answers were to be admired and filled up the mugs again.

A bleary and unshaven Siever woke us at dawn and a carrier arrived with some rations. The carrier driver was delighted to stay for breakfast with us and for champagne cocktails drunk out of a mess-tin. The Germans now saw what the Englander ate for breakfast and approved of bacon and eggs but were wary of the tea. Before I sent them back on the carrier the stocky one handed me his Luger which had the death's head and German eagle set in the butt-plates; I later gave this to Lieutenant Tony Brady when I left the army. Heels were clicked, salutes exchanged and they departed. Before I hear any howls of 'fraternising with Satan' from any non-combatant, trendy types, I advise them to go to the words of Christ: 'Who are you to judge another man's servant – by his own master he standeth or falleth'. Years later I heard that Jimmy Dunnill, our CO, when entertained as a prisoner by a German colonel was sent back with the comment: 'Do not judge the German army by what you see behind me'. I did recall at the time a line that Colonel John Horsfall wrote to me when he was a very temporary staff officer: 'I have come to realise one thing, Colin, the further back you go the lower the type.'

Chapter 23

The Mills of God

Everybody wants to surrender to 'English' soldiers and Lieutenant Colin Gunner takes the surrender of a Luftwaffe Division. At the same time he has his first meeting with the Bulgarians who are feared and hated by the Carinthians.

ALL PRISONERS departed and the train well looted, I declared a holiday for the boys and we lay sunbathing on the riverbank. Fishing lines of signal cable hung in the water attached to bottles of cooling champagne; a haze of tobacco hung in the still and sunny air. Peace was supreme even if I knew that, sooner or later, Jack, or that bloody adjutant, would arrive with orders. As I dozed half-naked on the warm grass Sergeant Hall called out: 'A German officer to see you, sir'. I opened my eyes and saw a very agitated and hot *Hauptmann* – captain – of German artillery standing there. Was I an officer?; I pointed to my shirt hanging on a bush; was I English?; I was not going to explain Irish Brigades fighting for England so merely said: 'Yes'. He drew himself up, saluted and said: 'Then I wish to surrender to you the 114th Luftwaffe Ground Division'. This was too much; SS battalions, Turcoman, Cossacks, but not *Divisions*, surely to God.

I tapped his shoulder and remarked: 'and when did a Hauptmann command a division?' He smiled and said: 'All the rest have run away. I am commanding what is left'. Feeling a touch peckish myself I ordered up some cold lamb and Siever hauled up the champagne. I invited him to join me while the fusiliers mumbled and chortled about the new *Officer's Mess*. McGee, who never could keep his mouth shut, was informed briskly that 'I run this bloody Platoon – not you'.

I was in no hurry so, after another refreshing snack, I asked the German where his *Division* was. It lay down the railway line about half a kilometre or so. I called Fusilier Smith, a tall and neat lad, and another like him, put on my shirt and belt, adjusted my caubeen at a stylish angle and off we went. We seemed to have gone a long way down that railway line seeing not a soul save one old forester, who bolted into the trees like a frightened stoat, so I informed the good Hauptmann that any funny business and I would shoot him without hesitation. He protested his virtue and rounding a hillock proved it.

There must have been about three thousand of them on the hillside. Cooking fires smoked and a babble of voices rose as we walked through them to a farmhouse. In the farm were about ten officers of different units and the Hauptmann must have said something about surrender to the English as a tall *Leutnant* in the *Gebirgsjaeger* (mountain troops) exclaimed: 'Gott Sie dank'. I muttered to the two fusiliers 'Put on the bull' and they stood as sentry at the door. We all sat at a long table and a trembling farm girl filled my glass from a jug of wine; a good beginning and a correct welcome for a member of Pat Scott's triumphant Irish Brigade.

Before we could enter into discussion a roaring of engines outside announced a motor-car and two motorcycle combinations arriving. The Alpine lieutenant, who spoke excellent English, exclaimed: 'The Bulgars'. Our door opened and a dirty, unshaven creature stood before me. He dripped gold braid and medals, wore a cocked-up Sam Browne and field boots, and must have been a full general at least. Before the Bulgar opened his mouth I asked the Alpine lieutenant if he could speak the other's language. He said he could so I asked him to 'inform the bastard that he salutes when he comes into my room'. This was delivered in a high-pitched snarl with obvious relish and *Groucho Marx* saluted in a flourishing fashion which would have earned him seven days in the Faughs. He then announced that he had come to take the surrender of all these Germans. Again the Alpine one snarled at him and, pointing to me, told Bulgar Bill that surrender had already been made to the 'great English Eighth Army'. I wish Monty could have seen that moment or, better still, Pat Scott. The Bulgar was obviously upset but stormed off with his guard of verminous thugs.

I then told the table to get their men into groups of two hundred, each under an officer or *Feldwebel* (sergeant) and simply march down the railway until they met the 'great English Eighth Army'. I was sure Murphy Palmer, our CO, would not be one whit surprised and would probably think they were the crowd leaving Punchestown Races. As a cunning afterthought I said that, in addition to all arms being handed over, all cameras had to be included. This caused no surprise and Alpine gave me a splendid Rolliflex. I told them to get a move on as Bulgar Bill would be back with reinforcements. They needed no warning on that score and I watched a *Feldwebel* literally kicking wounded men to their feet shouting 'march, march, mein Kameraden, or stay here for the Russians'. No parade I ever saw fell in so quickly or set off with such vigour. When the last trooper went down the hill the two fusiliers and I pounced on the camera pile. I dampened their spirits by saying: 'Now I'll do what I've always wanted to do – hold a camera parade'. Somehow we got the lot in sacks and started off back; if those bloody Bulgars had turned up the defence would have been Homeric.

On arrival back at the train I kept my vow. As I had discovered the treasure

I informed the waiting vultures that I would take three and Sergeant Hall two. Then, with his back to the queue, so that he could not spot his cronies, Siever would pass back one each. This was done in a fair fashion and I saved an excellent movie camera for Tony Morris and another for my favourite young villain, Corporal Keenan, now in another platoon. Miraculously we remained undisturbed by the Gods above save for more rations being sent up. *OK, fine*, said 11 Platoon, *leave us here a month, just see if we care.*

But now terrified civilians were coming in from the nearby farms begging for an 'English' soldier to stay with them. The Bulgarians and other banditi were loose on pillage and rape. I still have a pathetic note telling me that a farmer who had spoken with us only an hour earlier had been butchered, shot by Bulgarians. And in one farmyard I saw the raped body of a girl aged *twelve*. I was quite used to death's picture in most forms but a child's body with half a dozen bullet holes in it caused me to explode with blasphemous horror. The two fusiliers with me stood aghast and one broke into tears. I had no authority to do so but in at least six farms I sent two of my chaps to stay the night. I suppose there have been many grateful for the sight of a British uniform but surely none more from the soul than an old lady kissing the hand of an Irish lance-corporal addressing her as 'Ma'. I had never really felt hatred before, and never against Germans who had killed some of my best friends, but I felt it now for these sub-human animals.

Londoner Bob Hogan was one of the bravest men I ever knew. It was widely believed that he had been recommended for the VC when, as Mortar Platoon sergeant of the Rifles in North Africa, he had called down his own gunfire onto his own overrun position. He received a Military Medal and a commission on the field which is itself a high award. We had been friends for a long time although he flew into a violent rage at me when, on returning from leave, he found that his favourite sergeant, Elliott, had been killed in the Spaduro attack. As I had been the only surviving officer from that affair he blamed me. Hogan was old for a platoon officer, nearly twenty-eight I would guess, but I was always glad to see his craggy features and hear his rasping voice calling me 'a useless little bastard'. I christened him *Old Hickory* and when I cross the *river* I hope I shall see him to find out what the billets are like and how to get on the right side of the CO.

Hogan was the battalion machine-gun officer in Austria. As such he stood by one of his Vickers guns at a roadside one day watching the *Ustachi* being driven along to death by Tito's troops. The *Ustachi* were nominally Yugoslavs but had fought on the German side from the beginning. Now, with Tito's communists triumphant, they were to be slaughtered, and I mean *slaughtered.* The column seemed endless as they were driven over the Drau bridge to the Yugoslav side; men, women, children and babies in arms, all were starving but kept moving by Tito's men mounted on ponies and carrying the infamous steel-tipped Cossack whip, the *nagaika*, one blow from which will split a man's face open. They were using them freely. I was told that some died on the bridge with Father Dan present and I shudder to think what that wonderful man of God said and thought.

Hogan and I watched impassively until a man in field grey crashed down in the gutter at death's door. Hogan ordered two of his gunners to lay him on the bank, then pushed some rum down him. This revived him somewhat and Hogan exclaimed: 'He's not a Jug, he's a bloody German'. So he was, as the Ustachi troops had a number of German NCOs as instructors. Hogan moved very fast then and a sign, in German, was put at the side of the road: 'All German soldiers fall out here'. Hogan must have seemed like Christ the Saviour to several as they fell out and were given a drink of water and a Woodbine.

A Yugoslav officer complete with whip clattered up on his pony and screamed at the resting Germans like a hysterical whore. The Germans turned their eyes to Hogan. The Jug then made the mistake of screaming at Hogan and brandished his whip. Hogan spoke to the gunner behind the Vickers: 'If this bastard lifts that whip blow him out of that fucking saddle'. The gunner elevated the Vickers to aim square into the Jug's belly and put his thumbs on the triggers. There were more hysterical screams, then the Yugoslav turned his horse and cantered off. Neither he nor Hogan had understood a word of the other's language but a machine-gun at a range of ten feet needed no interpreter. About eighty Germans were collected in this way and sent back to a British PoW camp.

Hogan and I also stood in a farm doorway when a Bulgar came down the hill on a bicycle and fell off. Picking himself up he saw that his very first bicycle had a bent crank. Lifting a German *Panzerfaust* (bazooka) rocket from the ditch he was obviously going to use it to straighten the crank. Hogan smiled happily and said: 'I think we'll go behind the house'. This we did and a shattering roar sent pieces of bicycle and bent Bulgar on to roof-tiles. I had told Hogan of that little girl's body. Before we parted he said: 'I've heard about those cameras. Where's mine, you miserable sod'.

Near the bridge was a German machine-gun emplacement with a loaded Spandau mounted on a tripod. We heard with satisfaction that some Balkan playing with it had tripped the trigger and mown down a group of his chums; the Mills of God sometimes grind swiftly.

Chapter 24

The Faughs Across the Drau

A remarkable Battery Sergeant-Major and how the prisoners-of-war survived in Lavamuend. And yet more surrenders.

THERE WAS a prisoner-of-war camp near Lavamuend. It was not a big one and it housed mainly New Zealanders captured in the desert battles. Our first troops to enter were greeted by Battery Sergeant-Major Atkinson of the Royal Horse Artillery. Atkinson was a tall, handsome man whose brasses shone, whose starched shirt was ironed in knife-edge creases and who looked as if he shaved twice a day. He was the senior warrant-officer of the camp and, under the German commandant, was responsible for order and discipline. He was English and, I think, a Londoner.

While all the PoWs were packed off quickly for return into the arms of their brothers still in Italy in Freyberg's immortal New Zealand Division, Atkinson and one or two NCOs stayed to help us with 'local difficulties' so I heard from him the tales of PoW life in Austria. They had enjoyed a good life compared to some of the large camps in Germany and Poland, but food had always been their pre-occupation. Luckily they had been sent out to work on local farms and, in many cases, found their employers more pro-British than pro-German. In fact Atkinson told me that on several occasions he stood behind a German soldier in the village shop and saw him refused his request. When Atkinson made the same request he was served by the girl who made derogatory remarks about *der Bifki* (the Germans). Habsburg and Hohenzollern were still enemies to those good people of the Drautal.

The commandant of the camp was a German officer of 1914-18 vintage and the guards were lenient towards the prisoners. At all costs they had been desperate to stay as guards and not be sent to face the hordes of Asia on those wind and snow-lashed hills of the Russian front. Atkinson told me that the only rough time was when the military police swooped on the camp and turned it over in a search for wireless, tunnels and contraband. Then it was best to stand to attention and say nothing until they had departed. After their final visit the commandant paraded the prisoners and told them that the behaviour of the police made him 'ashamed to be a German officer'. He also paraded the entire camp some weeks before we arrived and taking his pistol from his belt handed it over to Atkinson in front of the parade as he, Atkinson,

147

was 'the new commandant'. BSM Atkinson, RHA, in his turn set his face for home but he left an indelible memory on some of us in the Irish Brigade. *If you can meet with triumph and disaster*; we were there meeting the triumph but I'll be damned if we met it with half the dignity that a WO of Horse Gunners had met his disasters over the years.

One of the last to leave was a New Zealand corporal and he begged Hogan and me to take him to an outlying farm before he departed. The only transport was a Bren carrier so, with myself as driver (and I was always convinced that I was the greatest carrier driver in Eighth Army), we loaded him aboard together with Lieutenant Michael Pattinson, who never had to be pressed into a party, and set off. It was a large and prosperous-looking farm but the reception was timid as I roared up to the door; until our New Zealander jumped down and fell into the arms of the family that is. Then, with weeping and laughter, the story was told. This was the farm where he had worked in darker times and he repeated time and time again that 'without these people I would not be alive'. What with the local fresh and potent wine and of course our own contribution of the hard stuff and cigarettes, it was an unforgettable evening and memorable for me as the youngest daughter of the house was not at all averse to a frolic in the hayrick with the youngest officer present – *me*.

When the time came to depart NZ stripped down to his underpants and vest and insisted that the family take everything he had in his poor world. We assured them that he would get a new outfit from the QM and then we too pitched in with all the cigarettes and cash we had on us. So, wrapped in a tatty blanket, one corporal of the old Desert Army parted forever from his 'enemy'. Another New Zealander told me that he looked down at the great bridge over the Drau many times and said: 'We'll hear the pipes and drums over there one day'. What he felt when Colonel Murphy sent the pipes and drums of the Faughs over that bridge I cannot conceive but I did feel that it was worthy of those great desert soldiers to have their exile ended by soldiers of the Royal Irish Fusiliers who had followed a similar march.

I took it into my head to inspect the hydro-electric set-up on the river and peremptorily ordered a resident and terrified engineer to escort me through echoing tunnels, silent turbines and rooms of dials. He considered my cigarettes generous payment. When I pointed to pylons with shattered porcelain insulators he explained that, lacking all other victims, the light-hearted British and American fighter pilots used them as targets. They must have been bloody good shots, I thought.

While I had been with the SS, Fred Lafferty had crashed into the Cossacks. Fred was a cheery, ebullient soul who commanded 10 Platoon of B Company and I did not catch up with him until we were all gathered in again as a battalion, but his accounts of balalaikas, vodka and hordes of horses gave me a pang of jealousy. Perhaps the best account would be from the Adjutant, Brian Clark, who took Prinz zu Salm, the Cossack commander halfway across Carinthia to bid farewell to his general, von Pannioitz. I heard that the Prince rode in on a thoroughbred hunter which caused that peerless judge of horseflesh, Murphy Palmer, to rub his hands with glee. More than that I do not know save that some of the liberated New Zealand PoWs helped to escort the Cossacks to our side of the Drau valley.

The whole world now knows of the horror when those Cossack thousands with their women and children were tricked into returning over the Hungarian frontier and there butchered by Russian troops. I am only grateful that my own Regiment was spared the filthy task of handing them over, if only for the fact that we would have faced that dread of all good regiments, *mutiny*.

A friend of mine in one of the units ordered to carry it out told me he 'never knew how many ways people could commit suicide' and that his major turned his back on his colonel remarking: 'I won't do it. Court Martial me if you wish'. This was a *political* decision resisted at all levels of army command and I will not have it said that it was a stain on the Colours of brave regiments. Even now the full story has never come out, but God have mercy on he who died with the decision on his conscience.

Chapter 25

Fraternization Time

Archie, the interpreter who lived in a castle, and the Doctor of Arnhem.

WHEN THE Irish Brigade arrived in Austria there were no German speakers at Brigade Headquarters; the limit of German at our level was *'wo ist der Schnapps?'* and, to any good-looking girl, *'Schlafen Sie mitt ...??'*. To overcome the language barrier Pat Scott *ordered* Archie to join the Irish Brigade as interpreter and general dogsbody. Archie was a tall, polite and bewildered boy who was colliding with the chiefs of the Irish Brigade in those frenetic days when Pat Scott was ordering Jugs, Cossacks, Bulgars and, for all he cared, Russians out of his brigade area.

I later joined Brigade HQ and got to know Archie well. I visited his home, the magnificent *Schloss Bleiberg.* crowning a fairytale village. Today Archie, *Doctor Graf Ariprand Thurn-Valsassina, Knight of Malta,* still lives in his beautiful castle with his beautiful princess and shoots stags, blackcocks and tourists (I hope!)

Visiting the *Schloss* I met all the family. His father, Alexander, was the personification of the Emperor Franz Josef; tall, immaculate, dignified and kindly, he radiated authority. Archie's mother electrified me. She had a vivacity that a girl of twenty would have envied, with energy beyond belief. I sat enthralled with tales of the Courts of Edward, Wilhelm and Paris and when she asked me 'Do you know how to call a Hansom cab?', put her fingers into her mouth and let out an ear-cracking screech, she won me over forever.

At tea one day sat a Polish captain, a French colonel, a Czech captain and myself. Without pausing in the middle of a sentence Archie's mother switched her language to whomever she was talking. I sat and marvelled and more so when she confided in me that Archie was not very bright as he only spoke *three languages.* Archie's sister, Christa, was of a beauty and status that only a semi-drunk officer of infantry could appreciate. My mind flew back, as I looked at Christa, to that moment on a dusty track in Sicily when that peasant girl stood watching the tired infantry filing past. Both were beautiful, both were beyond reach.

Archie told me the tale of his old governess. I believe she was a Scots-woman who had brought up Archie and Christa. Pensioned off, she lived down in the village in some small cottage. In the last days of the war some SS with armoured cars crashed into the Schloss; they were hard men and did not really care who lived or died. After demanding food and drink they departed to see, as they went down the village street, the Union Flag flying on the lawn of this invincible old lady. The column screeched to a halt and the officer glared at this brave woman flying the enemy colours. I would like to think that she shook her brolly at him and said: 'be off young man'. Instead, after a few seconds hesitation, the SS officer touched his cap and said: 'a few like you and *we* would have won'.

Later I took Archie from Brigade HQ to a very hilarious party with some Czech officers. Archie liked a party and was an asset at any. Among the Czech officers was a tall, black-moustached, striking figure. Archie glared at him; he glared at Archie; Archie said *'Kinski'*; he said *'Thurn'*. This Czech was a member of the great family *Kinski* whose palace stands today in Vienna. Archie and he were cousins.

The evening progressed and as long as my girl, Betty, stayed loyal to Colin Gunner I did not give a damn where Colin Hill or Michael Pattinson, both officers of the Irish Fusiliers, ended up. Archie, sitting beside me, suddenly became very formal and said: 'Look at Kinski, disgraceful'. Kinski was dancing the *mazurka* with some farm girl and doing it very well. His eyes shone, his black hair was tousled, his shirt ripped open. I admired him. Archie drew himself to his full height and thundered: 'Kinski! Remember who you are!' Then he fell flat on his face. When I took him home that night it took so long for both of us to get to the front door that I christened him *'The Rudderless Ship'*.

My affection for Archie and his family can never die and I hope that whistle for a cab was heard by Peter at *The Gate*.

Betty, the girl I had taken to the party had been the girlfriend of Terry O'Connor, the adjutant of the Skins. Going into the bar of the Post Hotel in Villach one evening I noticed Terry, Betty and two other Skins' officers at a table but was shocked when Terry marched up to the bar and said: 'I want a word with you – outside'. I searched my mind for any offence I could have given him, having always regarded Terry as a friend. Outside he smiled at my guarded and wary stare and said: 'I'm leaving the Army tomorrow. I want you to keep an eye on Betty.' Relief shot over me as, instead of a punch in the eye, he was asking me to supersede him with a very attractive and affection-ate girl. I hastily pointed out that even now he had two young and virile Skins' officers at his very table to which he snapped: 'I'm asking you'. We marched back together and I took Betty off to the Officers' Club at Maria Woerth with Terry's blessing and filthy stares from the two panting ones. I believe that

Terry spent that last night being put to bed by the warriors of his old platoon in a flood of nostalgia.

Betty and I lived quite happily for many months and Danny, my batman, a clean and quiet young rifleman, at Brigade HQ, always knew when to bring in two coffees when he woke me up; but only one with cognac. Betty was secretary to the *Herr Direktor* at the *Zivil Krankenhaus* (hospital) in Villach and, collecting her there one evening, I noticed an armed sentry at one door. In the jeep I asked Betty 'why the soldiers?' She replied: 'Oh, an SS doctor is under guard, he is my cousin'. This intrigued me, so next day I went into the room and saw a handsome blond Austrian of about twenty-seven in sports coat and slacks. *Was he a doctor?* Yes. *Was he Betty's cousin?* Yes. Was he SS? Yes. *Why under guard in a hospital?* Because he was SS and had been in for a minor operation.

Then, out of the blue, he said: 'I don't know why I should be under arrest. I saved your wounded at Arnhem. Colonel Warrack of your parachute troops knows me and will testify on my behalf'. I wrote to Colonel Warrack, who was then in Palestine with 6th Airborne Division, and he wrote back confirming all that Egon Skalka had said. Yes, he had come into the airborne lines when all was lost and evacuated the wounded; he had undoubtedly saved British lives; he had behaved as a doctor should.

Later, on leave, I traced Colonel Guy Warrack to his home in Edinburgh and he told me the tale over excellent sherry. Warrack was one of those fine men who stayed with the many wounded and went into captivity with them. Later he escaped and later still wrote a splendid book about those disastrous days. He did not know it but, as I studied his face and listened to his voice, I was thinking of another great Scottish doctor, our own Hunter Lang, killed in action as he tended the stricken at the Battle of the Sangro. Warrack said Skalka only peeved him once as, when driving him away in a captured airborne jeep, he pressed a packet of captured Players upon him. I never mentioned anything to higher powers but gave Skalka the letter and details.

One night I did a fool trick which, had it misfired, would have got me into real trouble. Skalka's home was in Klagenfurt and he had not been there for many months. After several nourishing brandies in the Mess I collected Betty and then told Skalka that, if he gave me the word of a German officer that he would return with me, I would take him to visit his parents at home. He gave me his word so, telling the guard that he was wanted at HQ, I took him home. When Betty and I went to collect him several hours later his parents embarrassed me with their gratitude while Skalka showed me an autographed photograph of Bittrich, the victor of Arnhem.

As he climbed into the jeep with us I grew reckless and, on the way back, stopped at an Allied Officers' bar. I told Skalka to say he was a Pole in civilian clothes and we all went in. The place was run by a Buffs officer whom I had last seen falling into the drums at a mammoth party at Campobasso. Still celebrating his survival as a rifle company officer he not only welcomed me but stood drinks all round. Skalka played up well, Betty was hysterical with giggles and the Buffs officer engrossed in somewhat blurred reminiscence. We all got home safely and, as I handed Skalka back to the guard, I hoped that all would come well for him. He clicked his heels, bowed and thanked me for his 'night out'.

I would love to know his fate.

Chapter 26

Goodbye the Faughs

The old army dies; the end of the Irish Brigade.

MY FRIENDSHIP with Archie and the incident with Skalka, the doctor of Arnhem, happened after I had been moved from the Faughs to Irish Brigade HQ. That move was one of many changes that, for me at least, signalled the end of the wartime army and the return to a peacetime organisation. The process was long and slow and at times it was almost unnoticed. The first sign was that the Faughs had to send six officers to join our 2nd Battalion in Palestine: those with the shortest overseas service suffered this fate. They were dined out in Faugh A Ballagh style and only Regimental officers will know what that means.

The dinner was memorable because of a speech made by a young priest, Father Sean Quinlan. Father Sean was one of two young priests hijacked, willingly, from the Irish College in Rome by Father Dan Kelleher. Dan had simply enlisted them into the Irish Brigade, dressed them as officers, stopping short of the pips, and made them members of the Mess. If it had been done by anyone other than Father Dan there would have been swift official reaction but by then even Field Marshal Alexander would have been pushed to contain this *turbulent priest* and great soldier of God.

Murphy Palmer, our CO, had a marvellous sense of humour and a great regard for our priests. Perhaps that was why, at this dinner, he baited Father Sean Quinlan into getting up to make a speech. Father Sean did just that and before he had uttered two sentences that table was hushed like a church. I can still remember his closing words across the arch of the years: 'And so I leave you, but never to forget your friendship and kindness, and to remember forever your green hackle which I have had the honour to wear.' I suppose I have heard my share of after-dinner spouters, and mostly drivel they were, but this speech from a young priest to about thirty battle-hardened officers of a crack regiment, all in various stages of drink, was incredible.

Father Sean sat down to thunderous applause and the best tribute was from a friend sitting opposite, a heavily decorated major and certainly no Catholic. His eyes met mine and he simply uttered 'Christ!'. The dinner was also memorable for me in another sense. Whilst entertaining my friends to a rib-cracking imitation of Colonel Murphy, I was seized by him and his thug of an adjutant and flung into the semi-frozen lake. Discipline restored, they returned to the Mess to order in the pipers yet again.

I too returned to the Mess and restored myself with a tumbler of neat arrak. We also had a small orchestra of Austrian civilians who played Strauss and Lehar during dinner. After dinner they were oiled up on liquor and then ordered to play the battle-hymns of Hitler's legions starting with the *Horst Wesel*. Any listening civilian must have wondered who had bloody well won. Perhaps, deep down, that orchestra enjoyed it.

Arriving now was a batch of young, newly-commissioned Second Lieutenants, some with Regular Commissions and family connections. I was sorry for them in one sense as some would complete a full life as a soldier without knowing what their reaction would have been to an enemy shell landing near them. An officer of ours who had *not* fought with us told me one night that he had applied for a Regular Commission in the Faughs. I burst out laughing and pointed to three of the young new arrivals with the words: 'You bloody fool, it's *their* army now'. I added that *my* army had ended when the last 25-pounder shell sailed over my head to burst on the front. He took this very badly but he did not get a Regular Commission. In another brigade a major with three Military Crosses applied for a Regular Commission. Badgered at the Interview Board he stormed out with the remark: 'You damn fool, I've killed more Germans than you've ever seen'.

A certain major, famous for his bravery and hot temper, got into a scrap which was hushed up although details of it were known as gossip. Two of the new boys were discussing it at breakfast one day and, turning to the Colonel, one remarked: 'I think the Army will be a better place when all those like X have gone, don't you sir?' The reply was perhaps a good epitaph for the fighting soldiers of my Army: 'I don't know what trouble X has got into but I do know that he was there when the bugle blew and that's more than I can say for *some people*'.

The 78th Infantry Division was to be broken up now and to mark its demise a full-scale ceremonial parade of the entire Division was ordered on a nearby airfield. This meant rehearsals and more rehearsals until turn-out and drill were perfect. Brian Clark was now in whatever paradise is reserved for infantry adjutants and he even achieved a little momentary popularity with the fusiliers at one rehearsal. In the absence of the RSM a most unpopular CSM was about to turn to the Adjutant and report the Battalion as present on parade. Instead he ordered a drill movement to be repeated, only to hear a bellow from the top of a large horse: 'I said hand 'em over, not drill 'em'. Waiting to join the parade I was in a good position to hear the chortles in the serried files.

After another rehearsal Colonel Murphy collected all the officers together and, from the saddle of his handsome chestnut, pointed out that all officers were to wear their Webley '38 Army issue revolvers and their belts. He pointed out that we were all sporting Lugers and 'You, Harry, haven't even got a pistol on at all'. This was addressed to a splendid Belfast character called Harry Quail whose pistol holster hung flat and empty on his belt. 'Oh, but sir I have', piped up Harry and, opening the holster, fished out a lady's handbag pistol about two inches long in mother of pearl. That brought the roof down before we dispersed to try to remember where our issue revolvers were.

It rained on another day and I had to endure listening to Corporal Patton, MM, behind me, pontificating to his friend Corporal Keenan on the imbecility of officers who dragged decent soldiers out into the rain to play at parades. I too was wet, as God did not hold some celestial umbrella over officers. I pointed this out to Patton and told him to shut up twice – then put him on a charge, the only time I had ever done that to one of my company: times were certainly changing. Next day he got a tongue-lashing from the company commander and then gave me a broad smile and a guardsman's salute outside HQ. Oh!, Patton, Keenan, Hall, Murphy, Taffy, McEvoy, Siever, Ostenelli, Salmon and McGee; we were parting now into another world. It was certainly a safer one but we were never again to know that moment when we looked at each other on a captured objective and felt a trust and bond that was never to come back. I see your faces now and hear you cursing rain, wind and snow as you toiled up Monte Grande, tired and laden.

When, on the great parade, the general called the nine battalions of infantry to attention he added: '*Remember the Fallen*' and as the Pipes played *The Flowers of the Forest* the ghosts fell in silently with the living. They had never been far away and are not far away even now. The bugles died away on that final soldier's farewell, *Last Post*, then screamed *Reveille*. As we prepared to march past the Army Commander the adjutant's horse, fed up with flies and heat, sat down to the destruction of that potentate's dignity. When Colonel Murphy roared 'kick him up, Brian' there was not a face in the 1st Battalion, Royal Irish Fusiliers that did not shine with delight.

At the end of the parade the Irish Brigade alone marched in column through the streets of Spittal and someone had had the imagination to hang boards across the tree-lined streets with the names writ large of all the battles from Algiers to Austria. Watching from his horse and surrounded by his colonels, Pat Scott, our Brigadier, knew what a very small handful of those magnificent battalions saluting him had seen it all. I believe *eight* captains or majors had stood at the head of B Company alone; God knows how many lieutenants were beside us.

A week or so after the parade my little world crashed to ruins. I was sent for by Colonel Murphy but instead of getting a rocket in his office he took me into the deserted Mess and, pouring two drinks, we sat in the empty room. He then told me that he wanted me to go as Liaison Officer to Brigade HQ and leave the Battalion. I was appalled and I think that brave Irish squire knew it as he added: 'You have a lot of friends there'. So that was it, I thought, telling Siever to pack my kit, chucked out of the home I had sought and sent away from the faces I knew. For forty-eight hours I hated Murphy's guts but after a week at Brigade HQ realised that he had done me the biggest favour I ever received in the Army and that the months ahead were to be the happiest I was to know, perhaps ever. Murphy left himself soon afterwards; Brian Clark was Staff Captain at Brigade HQ which put a dash of vitriol in my champagne, and my military deity, Colonel John Horsfall, was no longer at the head of his beloved, brave Riflemen to whom he had returned for a time in Austria.

In the smoke and the dust of that last shellburst were faces and memories that live for ever; intangibles that no money, drink or women could ever compare with. I only give my gratitude to God that I marched with the Faughs in the greatest fighting Brigade that ever left Britain's shores.

Glossary

Adjutant	The officer responsible to the Commanding Officer for the smooth running and discipline of a battalion. Brian Clark was one of the best.
Bren	The standard British light machine-gun. (Derived from a Czechoslovakian weapon and modified by its British manufacturers; the name includes the first two letters of the weapon's towns of origin, Brno in Czechoslovakia, and manufacture, Enfield in England.)
Carrier	An open-topped, tracked vehicle, armoured against small-arms fire. Designated the Universal Carrier but better known as the Bren-gun carrier. The author's platoon of the Kensingtons had eight of these to carry their four Vickers MMGs, sighting equipment, crews and 36,000 rounds of ammunition.
CCS	Casualty Clearing Station.
CO	Commanding Officer (of a battalion).
CSM	Company Sergeant-Major (Warrant Officer II).
Gharri	An Egyptian horse-drawn cab.
GMC	An American heavy lorry.
Fixed line	The line of fire of a machine-gun set up in a fixed position.
Focke Wulf	German aircraft – in the context of this book these were fighter aircraft.
Kangaroo	Armoured personnel carrier, converted from Sherman tank or 'Priest' self-propelled gun.
Luger	German automatic pistol, much sought after by Allied troops.
Mark IV	German medium tank.
Nebels	Nebelwerfer, six-barrelled German rocket launchers: inaccurate but lethal.
OCTU	Officer Cadet Training Unit.
OP	Observation Post.
PIAT	Projectile, Infantry, Anti-tank: British spring-loaded anti-tank weapon.

Rifle Company	One of the sub-units of an infantry battalion.
Sangar	A protective rampart of stones
Schmeisser	German sub machine-gun.
Sherman	American tank.
Spandau	German machine-gun.
Verey light	Signalling flare fired from a flare-pistol.
Vickers	The standard British medium machine-gun from 1914 to 1962. Capable of engaging targets at over 4,000 yards, it was issued to infantry battalions, such as the Kensingtons, were designated as machine-gun – or support – battalions. These had 48 Vickers MMGs each but the Kensingtons were among a number which also operated 4.2 inch mortars.
88	The German 88mm anti-aircraft gun, also used with great effect as an anti-tank and field gun.
105	The German 105mm field gun.

An infantry *battalion* in action comprised about 500 fighting men, commanded by a lieutenant-colonel. It was divided into four fighting – or rifle – *companies* each of which was commanded by a major or captain; the strength of a company varied but was rarely more than about 80 men. A company included three *platoons* of about 25 men each, commanded by a lieutenant or, often, a sergeant. Three battalions formed an infantry *brigade*, commanded by a brigadier: the addition of supporting units from Royal Artillery, Royal Engineers, Royal Signals etc. created a brigade group. A *division*, commanded by a major-general, normally contained three brigades.